Metaverse Investing Guide for Beginners:

Top 5 Unique Strategies to Create Wealth in Metaverse. Why Metaverse Will Create More Millionaires Than Anything Else. Altcoins, NFT, DeFi, Blockchain Gaming

"Your investment should be equally risky and rewarding."

— Anuj Jasani

Disclaimer:

The contents of this book may not be reproduced, duplicated or transmitted without direct written permission from the author.

Under no circumstances will any legal responsibility or blame be held against the publisher for any reparation, damages, or monetary loss due to the information herein, either directly or indirectly.

Legal Notice:

This book is copyright protected. This is only for personal use. You cannot amend, distribute, sell, use, quote or paraphrase any part or the content within this book without the consent of the author.

Disclaimer Notice:

Please note the information contained within this document is for educational and entertainment purposes only. Every attempt has been made to provide accurate, up to date and reliable complete

information. No warranties of any kind are expressed or implied. Readers acknowledge that the author is not engaging in the rendering of legal, financial, medical or professional advice. The content of this book has been derived from various sources. Please consult a licensed professional before attempting any techniques outlined in this book.

By reading this document, the reader agrees that under no circumstances are is the author responsible for any losses, direct or indirect, which are incurred as a result of the use of information contained within this document, including, but not limited to, —errors, omissions, or inaccuracies.

Table of Contents

Introduction

What do you imagine when you hear the word Metaverse? Perhaps, the first thing that comes into your mind is a scene in a sci-fi movie where people are communicating, working, and living in a virtual space with modern gadgets. Well, what you envision is coming real soon!

In fact, the early stage is happening right now across the internet-powered platforms. The gaming industry is scaling up its virtual realms and services. The tech companies are producing more advanced virtual reality gadgets and super-power computer hardware to prepare for the eventual advent of the Metaverse. Even e-commerce is scaling up its features to offer better shopping experiences. A lot is happening in the tech world now, triggering an excitement to experience this grand vision where we are not a bystander but inside this immersive world.

Let me share with you my book "**Metaverse Investing Guide for Beginners**: *Top 5 Unique Strategies to Create Wealth in Metaverse. Why Metaverse Will Create More Millionaires Than Anything Else.*

For users and consumers, the idea of the Metaverse can be both fascinating and overwhelming. This unknown territory may compromise our privacy, especially for non-techie individuals who prefer to live the traditional way.

Nevertheless, Metaverse is highly-anticipated because it will allow us to transcend from the physical world to the virtual world. We can work, shop, socialize, or connect wherever we are. Moreover, we can leverage the potential of the Metaverse to help us achieve our financial goals.

With the right mindset, preparation, and tools, you can start your dream business, create a stream of income, and gain profits from Metaverse investing. Like the real world, this parallel digital world will be providing jobs and income-generating opportunities that we can maximize to live an abundant life. The key to discovering these possibilities is to find the right tools that can fast-track our journey to becoming one of the new millionaires.

I've been through this journey and now enjoying the fruits of my crypto investing strategies. And I am very excited about the realization of the full Metaverse which can give us more doors to earn active and passive income. My new book "**Metaverse Investing Guide for Beginners**: *Top 5 Unique Strategies to Create Wealth in Metaverse. Why Metaverse Will Create More Millionaires Than Anything Else* can help you on your own journey to success.

I wrote this book for you to unleash your inner spirit and expand your horizon by leveraging the new investment frontiers. It can be your best tool to get ready for the Metaverse. Each chapter is designed to inform and equip you with knowledge about the Metaverse, its features, benefits, and elements.

In *Chapter 1 Metaverse the Future World,* I will take you back to where it all began, what it is all about, how it works in the current world, and what will it take to achieve the true Metaverse. You will also learn the stages of its realization, the risks and challenges, and more.

In *Chapter 2 Exploring the Potential of Metaverse*, I will help you better understand this new world. You will meet the early industry players and companies that are building the structural foundation to scale up their businesses. I've also listed the potential benefits and drawbacks of the Metaverse and how it can change our norms of living.

In *Chapter 3 The Role of NFTs in Metaverse*, I discussed everything you need to know about non-fungible tokens. NFTs are one of the pillars of the Metaverse.

In *Chapter 4 Blockchain, Cryptocurrency, and NFT Interplay in the Metaverse,* you will learn their crucial roles in the full realization of this concept.

In *Chapter 5 Guide to Metaverse Investing: Will You Be the Next Millionaire*, I shared information about available jobs and some creative ways to earn money in the virtual world. You will also learn why you have to invest in the Metaverse, how to invest, and what to watch out for.

In *Chapter 6 Creating Wealth in Metaverse: Strategy 1 Invest in NFTs*, I will assist you in exploring the benefits of investing in non-fungible tokens.

In *Chapter 7 Creating Wealth in Metaverse: Strategy 2 Buy Metaverse Tokens*, I talked about the types of tokens and the best ones to invest your money in.

In *Chapter 8 Creating Wealth in Metaverse: Strategy 3 Invest in Metaverse Platforms,* I listed down the elements you need to check out when selecting a Metaverse project and the top platforms to consider.

In *Chapter 9 Creating Wealth in Metaverse: Strategy 4 Invest in New and Upcoming Projects,* I recommend the most promising platforms that are getting a lot of interest from investors right now.

In *Chapter 10 Creating Wealth in Metaverse: Strategy 5 Leverage the Opportunities of Real Estate,* I talked about some real estate jobs in the virtual world.

At this juncture, I wish that you will find what I've written helpful in comprehending the concept of the Metaverse. It pays to be prepared and informed about this incredible new world that aims to fuse into our physical world.

Like you, I am waiting for its complete manifestation and to give us the ultimate experience of cross-border realms. What we can do right now is to maximize the early opportunities to earn the companies that are investing in Metaverse projects and related products. Start investing in Metaverse now and enjoy the road to becoming a millionaire.

I tell you, this is a chance of a lifetime. So, let's invest and enjoy Metaverse to the fullest!

Chapter 1

Is Metaverse the Future World?

"Today, I think we look at the internet, but I think in the future you're going to be in the experiences." Mark Zuckerberg

Is Metaverse the next frontier and iteration of the Internet? A portmanteau of "meta" and "universe", the Metaverse allows a crossover from the physical realm to the virtual world.

We all know that the advent of the Internet has altered the traditional landscape of commerce, business, technology, communication, and lifestyle. Its development has fueled modern technology and devices, making it one of the greatest human inventions.

When Facebook rebranded its company as Meta in October 2021, the tech and social media went buzzing about Metaverse. Overnight, the interest in this futuristic idea swept the industry and many people turned into Metaverse experts.

Big companies in various industries began planning to realign their investments and support the major players who want to build the future of Metaverse.

Chapter Summary

- Where did it all begin?
- What is Metaverse?
- How does Metaverse work?
- Key stages of Metaverse
- What does it take to build the Metaverse?
- Challenges and Risks
- Is Metaverse the Web 3.0?
- Is Metaverse already happening?
- Takeaways

The Metaverse fever didn't begin with Facebook's rebranding. For decades, there are platforms with an existing virtual reality world that can be accessed through techie gadgets like the VR headsets.

The subsequent proto-Metaverse platforms include the popular games Fortnite, Roblox, Animal Crossing: New Horizons, Minecraft, and World of Warcraft. They have been using avatars, hosting online events, and engaging in world economies.

However, these platforms offer limited capabilities and only display a standalone Metaverse of their own.

The real Metaverse is the next level.

Where did it all begin?

Metaverse was once a far-fetched concept that we may never imagine materializing soon. This fictional virtual world was introduced by American author Neal Stephenson in his 1992 novel "Snow Crash."

The Metaverse in the story appeared like an urban environment on a 100-meter wide road which Stephenson referred to as the Street. It was an undeveloped avenue that allowed participants to make their own 3D buildings, structures, mini-streets, signs, special neighborhoods, and even free-combat zones. The three-dimensional space was accessible through personal terminals and VR goggles.

The futuristic life-like avatars in the story and other digital reality features have sparked the interest of the gaming products developers, architecture, fashion, design, and other related industries. Soon afterward, Oculus Quest and VR headsets models were released in the market and become widely popular to access virtual games.

Stephenson wrote:

"A speech with magical force. Nowadays, people don't believe in these kinds of things. Except in the Metaverse, that, where magic is possible. The Metaverse is a fictional structure made of

code. And code is just a form of speech- the form that computers understand. The Metaverse in its entirety could be considered a single vast Nam-Shub, enacting itself on L. Bob Rife's fiber-optic network."

So, what exactly is Metaverse?

The Metaverse is an integrated network or social sphere that operates in the digital space. It is a continuum of several immersive virtual experiences in the digital spaces. All the synchronous experiences enhance the sensation of interactions. It is far better than the present feed-based social media video calls.

The closest way to explain a Metaverse experience is through video games. These games utilize 3D virtual reality features to deliver immersive experiences to users.

Most of them have elements and services that are already crossing over the aspects of our lives. Roblox, for instance, has been hosting virtual meetups, concerts, and events for its users.

Users of the Metaverse or augmented reality world would meet and socialize with other participants using personalized avatars in real-time. The different range of activities is accessible using specialized devices like virtual reality headsets, smartphones, digital glasses, goggles, and more.

In short, the Metaverse is an embodied internet that provides a scaled-up world in the virtual space. Just like the world where we are in, it is a place where we connect with our families, friends, work colleagues, clients, and other significant people.

Other functions of the Metaverse:

- Provides a remote platform where a group of individuals socializes, works, talks, and virtually does anything

- Allows active interaction and strong connection regardless of each other's location

- Interconnecting different platforms just like what the internet is doing- allowing the users to access multiple websites with a single browser

- Offers the things we want to experience with other people- hanging out, playing games, attending events, watching concerts, dating, shopping, working, accessing educational opportunities, visiting remote locations, and a whole lot more

- Uses the technologies behind virtual reality (VR), augmented reality (AR), holographic avatars, spatial video and audio, and other forms of communication

- Delivers functions that enable groups of people to collaborate for better productivity or host activities to conduct business

For instance, real estate companies can offer virtual property tours to prospective clients and investors. Remote teams can plan and discuss important matters seamlessly wherever their individual locations are. Users and consumers can easily access the immersive digital content using smartphones or digital glasses.

Metaverse also provides an immersive environment where the computing world is embedded in the physical realm and vice-versa. The fusion results in the creation of a new platform layer that allows transcendence and interactive connection among humans.

This simulated digital space mimics the real world and allows users to choose how to experience this simulated reality. As it continues to grow, Metaverse offers an alternative virtual space where we and others co-exist, just like the real world.

How does Metaverse work?

Metaverse is an around-the-clock shared virtual environment with immersive features gaming, online shopping, or social interactions. At its infancy stage, the Metaverse content uses game-style graphics and avatars. But its great potential is slowly unfolding.

The radical change in the paradigm will be leveraging and converging all the available technologies. It promises no limitations of accessibility and more expansive activities that bring in ultimate experiences.

The duo of blockchain and cryptocurrency will be shaping the next-generation Web 3.0 as an open network that allows composability and interoperability. We need to understand that the concept of composability is crucial for the exponential growth of the Metaverse as the concept aims to be open source and accessible to developers anywhere in the world.

Stages of Metaverse

Stage 1

This is the initial stage which is what we are currently experiencing. It is about 50% immersion in the virtual world. It can be experienced using a 2-hand controller and a headset. The present VR influences hearing and sight, with a limited sensation of touch.

At this stage, the blockchain protocols in the Metaverse games like Counter-Strike, Fortnite, and GTA are influential in the development of Web 3.0's infrastructure layer. These include Ethereum, Tron, Polygon, Solana, BSC, and Cardano.

Non-fungible tokens (NFTs) are also leveraging the opportunity for people to gain ownership of digital assets, real estate properties, in-game currency, artworks, skins, clothes, guns, and spaceships.

The decentralized nature of these Metaverse-like platforms also allows the participants to get a revenue share or cast a vote on certain matters like fees, grants, or auctions. Users spend and earn money in Metaverses through buying and selling, advertising, offering tickets for virtual events, real estate transactions, and creating NFTs. All these activities play a huge part in the growth of a Metaverse platform.

Popular examples

> The Sandbox Metaverse platform and rapper Snoop Dogg collaborated in the creation of Snoopverse. Their project showed a virtual version of his mansion which he used to host concerts and parties. The success of the project has led to the popularity of Sandbox, attracting $359 million of industrial investment which includes Soros Fund Management and Winklevoss Twins.

➢ Roblox users can create mini-games and then sell them in exchange for the Robux. Tokens can be converted for fiat currency of your choice. There was one user who wanted to become Snoop Dogg's virtual neighbor and purchased a plot of land worth $450,000 to achieve his goal.

➢ CEO of Bluzelle Pavel Bains and Executive Producer of play-to-earn MixMob game that uses Solana blockchain said that they are selling in-game NFTs. There are also MixBots, masks, and other items for entry-level players and upgrade purposes. With the success of the game, investors had their eye on MixMob. The recent additions are DeFinance Capital, IOSG, Not3lau Capital, and Ascentive Assets.

➢ CEO Justin Lacche who has four minor league sports teams that compete both in physical and Metaverse fields said *"And because it's decentralized, it can't be hacked because there's nothing centrally to hack."* This allows the sports team to sell real-world goods like posters, t-shirts, NFTs, and other paraphernalia.

Co-founder of NFT marketplace Aaron Barbieri-Aghib AarnDime affirmed the potential of Web 3.0. *"It promises a world where users won't rely on massive centralized companies and instead will maintain control over their personal data."* But he added that to reach this goal, people need to use Metaverse every day. Even if the concept is cool, a lot of people would not embrace the concept if it is not intuitive and is difficult to use.

Stage 2

This stage is about 80% immersion in virtual reality. We will have easier access to tools, apparel, shoes, bodysuits, and omnidirectional treadmills that help us experience being in the Metaverse. There will be applications that provide some real-life sensory experiences like the sense of touch and full-body movements. Unfortunately, the sense of taste and smell will not still be available.

During this time, Decentralized Autonomous Organizations (DAOs) will dominate the scene when it comes to funding, decision-making, upgrading, and implementing reforms to the Metaverse.

Anyone can participate while the developers can do freelance work if they are up to it. As jobs in the Metaverse become more common, the result will be full interoperability.

This means that we can go from one Metaverse to another Metaverse and buy, sell, or exchange assets. It's like being in the physical world where we can go from one store to another when searching for the items we want to purchase.

Stage 3

This is the Advanced Virtual Reality stage where tech companies would be introducing products that send direct signals to the brain for active immersion. There is no need for us to access the user interface to enjoy the experience.

Neuropathic VR will be a common thing during this stage, transporting the human consciousness to any Metaverse that offers identical sensations to the real thing.

Stage 3 offers full immersion, where we will find it hard to distinguish if we are in the Metaverse or the real world. It becomes a part of our daily life, where people can hang out, meet, and do activities together. Virtual governments may also exist, making people Metaverse citizens.

Getting married and enjoying a relationship will also be possible in the Metaverse. There will be massive development of artificial intelligence (AI), creating models with human-like emotions and consciousness.

If all of these manifest, there will be a reduction in carbon dioxide emission as travel declines. It may also influence the downtrend of the crime rate worldwide.

Stage 4

Stage 4 is when the real world and Metaverse are completely indistinguishable. Using advanced neurotechnology, we can easily map out the mind or upload one's brain to the Metaverse to access data or information. This breaks down the human body's limitations, liberating us from laws and borders.

With Metaverse in full swing and incorporated into the physical realm, there are no boundaries to what our mind and body can do. By using AI technology to augment the experience and enhance our mental capabilities, we can easily go back and forth between the parallel worlds.

What does it take to build the Metaverse?

Unlike other virtual reality ideas that are embodied in the apps, developing a Metaverse is more complicated. It is not created using the agile development model that is commonly used today.

To create a complex virtual space, it is important to make interconnecting layers such as infrastructure, human interface, spatial computing, decentralization tools, user experiences, creators economy, and content engine drivers.

- *Infrastructure* involves GPUs and connectivity technologies such as Wi-Fi, 5G, and cloud

- *Human interfaces* are devices and technologies that will help users to leverage the benefits of the Metaverse such as headsets, haptics, AR glasses, and more

- *Spatial computing* refers to modeling frameworks and 3D visualization
- *Decentralization elements* include blockchain, edge computing, AI, and other democratization tools

- *User experiences* involve skills in digital apps for work, gaming, shopping, or events

- *Creator's economy* is the selection of digital assets, tools for design, and e-commerce shops

- *Content engine drivers* help in fostering engagement such as social media, reviews, ads, and ratings

Challenges and Risks

Challenges

The ideal Metaverse is decentralized, open, and with no single entity that can control the users' assets and data. It is slowly manifesting but its full development may take a longer time. Also, the fact that its early stage of development is dominated by giant service providers and tech companies may compromise the goal.

The *centralized nature* of companies like Facebook, which recently rebranded itself as Meta has been storing the users' content and digital identities on their servers. This represents their ownership of the data and decision-making ability. Sadly, many tech companies are poor custodians of these data, hence the need to wait for Web 3.0's new set of rules and guidelines.

For now, observing how technologies that support Web 3.0 and the Metaverse are evolving and transforming the platforms is the best thing we can do. Seeing how Metaverse's creator economy can supplement Web 3.0's vision of developing a new financial world with decentralized solutions is fascinating.

As the Metaverse develops further, the open-source public chain and interoperability of Web 3.0 are crucial to the merging and interlinking of the physical and virtual worlds. They should not only support each other but overlap in a smooth, seamless way.

Another challenge for the tech industry is the urgent need to create super-computers to support the Metaverse.

As an example, *Intel* said that it is now developing processors that are 1000 times more powerful than today's models. Their expert teams are also working on hardware improvements, software architectures, and new algorithms for more immersive computing that will leverage the next generation of the internet and the Metaverse.

Risks

There are several risks we need to consider when dealing with the Metaverse.

- **Platform's value** – The value of the Metaverses greatly depends on their popularity, proprietary cryptocurrency, and services. If they fail to sustain the interest of users, the value of related assets falls drastically.

- **Decentralized governance** – While this element is seen as a positive element of Metaverses, it can be a form of bug that hinders some users in the decision-making. Security breaches and hacking can put the investment and data in massive danger. It is important to choose a Metaverse with secure and tight security measures to compromise the privacy of users.

- **Learning curves** – Like any other project, the Metaverse has peaks and curves. It is crucial to understand the cycles and leverage them to our advantage while the platforms are continually developing the features to sustain their growth.

Is Metaverse the Web 3.0?

Web 1.0 was yesterday's internet. It existed between 1991 and 2004 when people who consumed it were more than the number of content creators.

Web 2.0 is today's internet, where creators dominated the platform and people interact through social media like Facebook and online platforms like YouTube. We post, comment, and share images and videos.

In Web 2.0 that we are utilizing now, we cannot monetize and control shared content. The platforms we are enjoying are highly centralized and controlled by big players in the tech and business industries. These companies are also developing and selling products or services in a centralized manner. They own our content on their platforms and control our creations.

To use their platforms and services, we need to register, provide our private data, and accept their terms and conditions. When they want to block or ban us from using their platforms, they can do it without our consent.

Even the gamers worldwide which are estimated to be over 2.5 billion do not own the in-game assets despite paying for them with real money.

But as the technology advances and developers become more creative, Web 2.0 is quickly evolving into the next-generation concept of the internet or Web 3.0. This evolution is believed to allow users to own and control online content, creations, online identities, and digital assets. We can make content, control, and monetize it to our own advantage.

Web 3.0 will be open to everyone who wants to leverage digital services. We do not need to register before accessing the services of any platform. As sole custodians of our private data and content, it will be our responsibility to protect them.

Web 3.0's backbone would be blockchain technology. The blockchain's financial transactions would use cryptocurrency.

- Blockchain enables peer-to-peer networking. The decentralized nature of blockchain allows users to own the data and conduct independent business with other users. The full authority on how and when to share the data is returned to the users. The assigned private keys help users to access the account.

- Cryptocurrency is virtual money or token used for transactions, both online and in the real world. It is stored in an electronic or digital wallet.

This is an example of what the eventual transformation of Web 2.0 to Web 3.0 looks like:

- From a **centralized** system to a **decentralized blockchain**

- From **Chrome** to **Brave** (a fast browser that offers more privacy to users)

- From **Facebook** to **Steemit** (the rewards-based social blockchain platform where users get paid for their creations and curated content)

- From **bank** to **Metamask** (the crypto wallet that is powered by the Ethereum blockchain)

- From a limited liability company or **LLC** to a decentralized autonomous organization or **DAO** (a type of LCC where no one has major control behind decisions)

- From Amazon Web Services or **AWS** to InterPlanetary File System or **IPFS** (a peer-to-peer hypermedia protocol that powers the distributed web)

- Twitter has rolled out its NFT profile pic verification

Metaverse and Web 3.0

The Metaverse and Web 3.0 are not rival versions of the internet. However, when these two concepts reach their full potential, their functionalities can overlap. The technologies that empower and support Web 3.0 and the Metaverse are similar.

But saying that Metaverse is the next phase of the internet or Web 3.0 (an embodied internet) is not true.

Here are the reasons why:

- *Metaverse* centers on providing how users will experience the future of the internet. *Web 3.0* is about the decentralization of the internet.

- *Metaverse* is a virtual reality space. *Web 3.0* is a decentralized version of the web.

However, they will be complementing each other functionalities.

- *Metaverse* is about merging the virtual and physical worlds. *Web 3.0* is offering a new set of guidelines and rules that allow decentralization and ownership of data or content.

- The creators in the *Metaverse* supplement the vision of the enhanced *Web 3.0* to create a new financial world that offers decentralized solutions.

Metaverse

The Metaverse is powered by diverse technology like cloud infrastructure, applications, software tools, hardware, platforms, and user-generated content. At its core, Metaverse will be leveraging the use of mobiles, computers, and other traditional devices while using immersive virtual reality (VR) and augmented reality (AR) wearables.

It is a representation of how people would be using the internet in the future. The Metaverse will transform the users' experience from 2D to 3D, offering three-dimensional web content rather than clicking or flipping content on the devices' 2D screens.

The emerging dimensions would bring work, entertainment, social media, education, gaming, and other real-world activities into an all-in-one platform. For example, the online gaming 2D webpage becomes a 3D sphere where players use in-game avatars to walk around, interact, and compete with other users.

The Metaverse will display the following features:

- Massive scalability
- Real-time rendering
- Unlimited number of users
- 3D virtual environments
- Interoperable
- Synchronous
- Data continuity
- Individual presence
- Persistence

Web 3.0

The internet is evolving constantly and most of us are anticipating what the future holds for us. Web 3.0 is shaping up nicely because of the exponential growth brought by the DAOs, NFTs, and P2E (play-to-earn) games.

The early signs of Web 3.0 are the emergence of decentralized web browsers and the NFTs or non-fungible tokens. NFTs are unique digital assets that represent ownership of content like art, music, video clips, and more.

The massive potential of Web 3.0 and its applications as the new generation of the internet offer great advantages to users.

Rather than using centralized websites like Google or Facebook that own and monetize our data and content, Web 3.0 allows us to use blockchain-based search engines, social networks, and apps where we control our data.

Is Metaverse already happening?

No one can predict when will the grand Metaverse will materialize. It can happen at the end of this new decade or sooner due to the emergence of foundational elements. But it is safe to say that the future of the digital transformation is slowly unfolding and influencing several aspects of life.

It was like what happened in 1989 when the *World Wide Web (www)* was invented by Tim Berners-Lee. People were excited to see the possibilities that it would bring. Fast forward to today, we are enjoying the convenience of the internet. This is what Metaverse is doing right now.

As everyone awaits, more industries are getting curious about how the Metaverse can change the world. Futurists, investors, executives, and founders are staking their claims and exploring its great potential to bring more profit, better social connection, massive entertainment, and more.

The Metaverse is solidifying its presence in the physical realm. It is traversing across the technologies, gaming world, real estate and business industries, social media platforms, and virtual currencies. These factors have become the building elements of its realization while the Internet makes Metaverse a popular concept.

- ✓ *Gamers* are already enjoying the experience of the Metaverse features of the Animal Crossing: New Horizons, Fortnite, and Roblox games.

- ✓ *Crypto developers* are building Metaverse tokens and the creators in the world of arts are leveraging the power of NFTs. If you own cryptocurrencies or NFTs, you are into Metaverse experiences.

- ✓ *Industrie*s using digital avatars during work meetings or virtual parties are treading into the path toward the Metaverse.

The global health pandemic due to COVID-19 is also instrumental in shaping the early stage of the Metaverse. Businesses, industries, and consumers have shifted to online-everything mode, allowing virtual environments, digital assets, and remote experiences to gain momentum.

Essayist and venture capitalist Matthew Ball has described the metaverse as a framework of a connected life *"Instead, it will slowly emerge over time as different products, services, and capabilities integrate and meld together."*

Takeaways

- Metaverse has various iterations that can be navigated using mobile devices, computers, and wearable technology.

- It uses decentralized autonomous organizations (DAO) and cryptocurrencies for quick and successful applications.

- Current trends in the industry are shaping the Metaverse. It includes collecting and trading virtual assets, game advertising, leveraging blockchain use, and blending digital and real-world experiences.

- Metaverse has an immense potential that can change the Internet's landscape, but it is unlikely to replace the web.

- In the end, the goal of the Metaverse is to create a digital space where people can interact, do business, and enjoy entertainment.

Are we all ready for the Metaverse? It's time to explore this future realm.

Chapter 2

Exploring the Potential of Metaverse

"Every brand you see in the real world will be in the Metaverse to give you the experience of buying virtual goods in the virtual world."- Anuj Jasani

In the mid-90s when the Internet is just beginning, people were skeptical because of several obstacles like technology limitations, slow dial-up access, and other factors that affect the performance. But as the provider vigorously resolved the issues and the users embraced the technology, Internet has become one of the greatest tech innovations in the world.

Due to the advancement of technology, people are always looking forward to the latest concepts, apps, products, and services to make life more convenient and exciting.

The current buzz is the Metaverse. Its potential growth is expected to be exponential and life-changing. It is considered a whole new horizon that can bring new opportunities and possibilities to the daily lives via augmented reality technology.

Chapter Summary

- What makes Metaverse unique and attractive?
- To whom does the Metaverse matter?
- Who are the early Metaverse industry players?
- Top reasons why Metaverse has become a global hype
- Will Metaverse change the way of living in the future?
- Potential benefits and drawbacks of Metaverse
- Takeaways

What makes Metaverse unique and attractive?

The Metaverse has the element of decentralization where there is no particular ruler. Various companies will develop their own Metaverses but allow the users to create and follow their own policies through the Decentralized Autonomous Organization (DAO).

While there will be companies that will set their own rules, what is certain is the rapid advancement of hardware to ensure truly immersive Metaverse experiences.

To whom does the Metaverse matter?

- **The gatekeepers**. They are the companies that will financially benefit from the creation of Metaverses and the development of future VR and AR headsets. The fastest ones to materialize their objectives will definitely enjoy the massive advantages that this new concept promises.

- **The users of social networks**. They are us, people who utilize social media platforms for different purposes. Signing up for these networks requires us to provide personal information that is sometimes compromised due to the lack of security measures.

  In the Metaverse, the headsets are likely to gather the users' spatial data. It may raise new privacy issues, which is one of the factors that should be given utmost attention by the gatekeepers.

- **The advertisers.** The consumer internet of today generates income from subscription revenues and advertising.

Some models may still work in the nature of future Metaverse.

However, some experts believe that traditional business models like DeFi-powered will be returning.

But one thing is sure, the business models will influence the decision of the interested companies to participate in the future virtual reality realm.

The early Metaverse developers

The year 2022 ushered in with the pronouncements of big players in the industry that they are planning to navigate the potential of Metaverses, NFTs, and the crypto spheres. This prompted investors and users to study the performance of companies that are already offering Metaverse-like experiences.

We should also be aware of those firms that are only motivated by FOMO or fear of missing out. While many are serious about launching their own Metaverse, others do not have the capability to scale up their networks to the full potential of the new realm.

The rapid technology innovations are also modifying the landscape of the financial and investment industries. Bitcoin's blockchain technology initiated this reform when it went public in 2009. Soon after, various cryptocurrencies emerged with their own blockchain to compete with Bitcoin.

This same blockchain technology is responsible for enabling Metavese's data continuity and functionality.

Meta (former Facebook Inc.)

The decision of Facebook to change its company name to **Meta** triggered enormous curiosity about the concept of the Metaverse. Everyone is waiting for how this popular social media platform of Mark Zuckerberg will evolve into a Metaverse. As early as 2014, Facebook has already invested in virtual reality technology. It has acquired Oculus and is working to create digital avatars and VR headsets, allowing users to connect with others while working, traveling, or enjoying entertainment activities.

"We want to get as many people as possible to be able to experience virtual reality and be able to jump into the metaverse and to have these social experiences within that" Zuckerberg stated during his interview with CNET.

Facebook has outlined its plans to incorporate Metaverse into its platform within the next decade or two with the help of its global partners. It has forged a collaboration with the UK Colorintech for its Metaverse content creation competition. It is currently working side by side with Germany's Alte Nationalgalerie for inclusive XR experiences.

Facebook has also announced its AR/VR startup growth project in Israel as part of the company's mission in harnessing the potential of the Metaverse. It is also developing Facebook Horizon, an OASIS version of a virtual world where anything is possible and users assume a distinct persona. With the help of Oculus Quest 2 or Oculus Rift headgear, users can seamlessly enter the expansive digital space.

In 2021, the social media leader has already spent $10 billion in terms of technologies to build Metaverse. With its infrastructural elements, thriving creator economy, social media advertisement engine, and range of Oculus headsets, Meta can easily develop a Metaverse prototype within 2 to 5 years from now.

Microsoft

Software giant **Microsoft** has been developing apps with mixed and extended reality (XR). The extended reality (XR) will fuse the real world with virtual reality (VR) and augmented reality (AR). Microsoft's goal is to create a work-focused Metaverse that connects all its services and products in Mesh. Users can easily use Windows, Microsoft teams, and other VR services on the platform.

As of today, Xbox Live has been connecting video game players worldwide. This 2022, it plans to bring virtual avatars, holograms, and mixed reality to Microsoft Teams.

Another project the company lines up for this year is the creation of 3D-connected environments for workplaces and retail. It is also collaborating with the US Army to create AR Hololens 2 headsets.

Minecraft

Minecraft, also owned by Microsoft, is an enjoyable virtual sphere for kids and adults who enjoy building their own environment and creating digital characters. This digital Lego-like game features a number of configurations that allow players to do anything out of the 3D cubes or blocks in the virtual space. It has a survival mode where users need to gather resources to feed themselves and survive the deadly creatures' attack throughout the entire game.

One of the elements of a Metaverse is the capability to let users exist in the digital universe and live like in the real world. Minecraft has accomplished this requirement by giving the player significance within the Metaverse or the virtual environment. Players can create their personalized Metaverse and set a unique experience like building settlements, socializing with other players, assigning roles to their avatar, establishing a hierarchy, and surviving according to the mechanics of the game.

Lastly, Minecraft has access to the Oculus Rift which is synonymous with the Metaverse immersive gaming experience. In a gist, Minecraft in its right is an example of a Metaverse.

Roblox

Roblox offers immersive virtual experiences that give gamers a glimpse of what the future world looks like in the Metaverse. This platform with popular games created by independent developers is believed to be the most expansive and closest vision of the Metaverse. Users also spent dollars to acquire Robux, the site's virtual currency to purchase digital items for characters, weapons, hot air balloons, and hats.

According to Roblox chief executive and co-founder Dave Baszuchi, their goal is to reach billions of users in the coming years. He said that *"just like the mail, the telegraph, the telephone, text, and video are utilities for collaborative work, we believe Roblox and the metaverse will join these as essential tools for business communication."*

The proto-Metaverse of Roblox has earned $454 million in revenues during the second quarter of 2021. With over 43 million active users who logged in daily, the company is positive that its transitioning to the full Metaverse will be smooth.

Epic Games

Looking back when **Epic Games** was developing Fornite in 2017, the game with tower defense-style has planned to build a Metaverse realm. But this game where players fight zombies became so popular, turning itself into a global phenomenon. The company rushed in adding dance parties, voice chatting, and other social features in the Fortnite Battle Royale mode to provide a more exciting gaming experience.

To date, Epic Games is marketing Fortnite as an interactive game and as a Metaverse. According to the marketing VP Matthew Weissinger, *"It's more than a game. We're building this thing called the metaverse- a social place."*

CEO Tim Sweeney has approved the company's investment in building the Metaverse. Epic Games allotted a $1 billion fund to fuel growth opportunities.

Sweeney said it was difficult to define Metaverse, saying that *"The metaverse is not an App Store with a catalog of titles. In the metaverse, you and your friends and your appearance and cosmetics can go from place to place and have different experiences while remaining connected to each other socially."*

In 2018 and 2019, Epic Games' Fornite generated over $9 billion in revenues. The Unreal Engine is instrumental to the users' VR and AR experiences. Epic Games' successful ventures included Travis Scot and Ariana Grande concerts, Martin Luther King Jr.'s immersive reimagining of "I Have a Dream" speech, music debuts, and trailers of popular movies. Fortnite has also partnered with Balenciaga, Air Jordan, and NFL.

Furioos of Unity

Furioos of Unity is streaming real-time fully interactive 3D environments with the help of their GPU server infrastructure. The cloud-based streaming technology of Furioos makes sharing complex and interactive apps easy. With its multiplatform capability and accessibility to smartphones and other devices, sending and receiving video streams are quite convenient.

Users can embed the applications to any website by copying and pasting the Furioos iFrame to generate a shareable URL. It makes sharing any kind of 3D project with collaborators and clients virtually fast and seamless. Receivers just need to drag and drop the ZIP file with the application. Furioos will immediately locate the .exe file and then upload it at once.

True to its mission to develop powerful applications, Unity has launched the Mixed and Augmented Reality Studio (MARS). It lets the participants use the additional digital apps in the virtual space to create a mixed reality experience.

According to senior VP for AI Dr. Danny Lange and VP of tools Timoni West, the company supports the revolutionary Metaverses that are beginning to manifest in the real world. Hence, they are investing in the digital twin or the physical world's digital representations.

Lange and West believed that the digital twin would become the foundation of a giant Metaverse concept, where users easily move across different virtual spheres without glitches.

"It has to be easy to use. It has to be easy to create content and experiences. It also has to be easy for people to make a living from…. it's in our DNA, in our blood to continue this and bring it into the Metaverse as well."

The Sandbox

The Sandbox allows players to build a virtual world and play, buy & sell NFT assets or real estate properties with NFTs. These non-fungible tokens are digital tokens that are unique, non-interchangeable, and indivisible. In this realm, we will have true ownership of in-game assets and use digital currencies any way we want.

Decentraland

Decentraland is another early mover that signifies an intention to make Metaverse the core product. This fully decentralized virtual world is controlled via the DAO and operates in the Ethereum blockchain. Since 2017, this platform is steadily growing. To date, its highest-paid piece of property is recorded at $2.4 million.

Its cryptocurrency is called MANA. It can be used to buy lands, build and design structures, create scenes and challenges like art exhibits or concerts, purchase items like Avatar wearables and other items in the marketplace, and even gamble in the casinos.

In 2021, the digital real estate firm Republic Realm purchased 259-parcel of land in NFT form. It was worth 1.2 million MANA or equivalent to $900,000.

Niantic

Pokemon Go of Niantic is one of the key platforms that deliver immersive experiences that cross the lines of real and virtual worlds. It has raised about $300 million to initiate its Metaverse project. Niantic aims to create an alternative to the "dystopian nightmare" notion of the Metaverse.

Apple

Apple could be a dark horse in the Metaverse race due to its mass-market adoption capability.

It can easily do what it has done to tablet and smartphone markets.

It is currently in the process of producing an advanced VR gear that is believed to revolutionize how users experience the Metaverse. It is also investing in AR hardware which is a sign that its App Store wants to be on the bandwagon when the digital revolution manifests its full potential.

JPMorgan Chase & Co.

JPMorgan Chase has taken the initial steps to explore Metaverse when it created the Onyx Lounge, the 3D browser-based virtual platform in Decentraland.

In a statement, this financial giant said *"The metaverse will likely infiltrate every sector in some way in the coming years, with the market opportunity estimated at over $1 trillion in yearly revenues."*

Pricewaterhouse Coopers

Metaverse platform Sandbox released a statement last December that the Hong Kong office of **Pricewaterhouse Coopers** has set up a virtual site to provide advice to those interested in exploring the potential of the Metaverse.

Walmart

Last December 2021, Walmart has filed new trademarks to manufacture and sell virtual items like toys, personal care products, electronics, sporting goods, and home decors. The company also released a statement that it would be offering NFTs and cryptocurrencies to users.

McDonald's

MacDonald's Corporation filed also files Metaverse-related patent applications to operate an online virtual restaurant with a home delivery service.

Nvidia

Nvidia is not a direct player but is seen as a key enabler of the Metaverse. It announced in 2021 that Ominiverse Enterprise would be combining 3D graphics with supercomputing and artificial intelligence (AI) to lay down the foundation of the Metaverse.

Top reasons why Metaverse has become a global hype

The first generation of services that use avatars is not considered Metaverse. It is because these platforms use a single app. To be categorized as

Metaverse, the platforms should have a multitude of loosely-tied services that provide a variety of real-time interactions.

The concept of the Metaverse is linked with the emerging Web 3.0 or the open-source and decentralized version of the internet. It would be using real-time 3D (RT3D) objects and engaging with available data.

The large collection of network services is interconnected, showcasing the dedicated roads that are built by the companies for their services. It is where we beat the paths to go from one place to another.

Here's a quick look at the features and advantages of Metaverse:

1. Democratized architecture and operations

With a democratized architecture, the Metaverse platforms are not owned by a single entity, group, or institution.

Holders of the platform's cryptocurrency have a right to engage in the network's decision-making. This means that it is no longer possible to make algorithm changes without the consent of the users.

2. Open-source

Since open-source is one of the key elements of the Metaverse, builders need to make their source codes available to everyone.

Global tech players are required to make their technologies, AI, and image synthesis accessible to help developers, startup companies, and other interested parties who want to develop their own platforms.

3. Advance scientific research

With more upscale simulation capacity, Metaverse can easily advance scientific research in different fields including aerospace, healthcare, and manufacturing.

Medical professionals can meet with the stakeholders virtually to present a simulated molecular structure of a new drug or vaccine.

Moreover, the Metaverse features can easily boost the success rate, error detection, and approvals of projects.

4. Revolutionize communication and interaction

At present, we are using the two-dimensional format when accessing online information. It involves visuals and texts, a 2D screen, and other input peripherals that allow us limited interactivity.

The realization of the Metaverse is regarded as a major input-out exchange revolution. With the help of hand controllers, voice commands, and eye-tracking features, we can easily interact with the visualized data.

5. Empower people with disability

In Metaverse platforms, people living with a disability can experience what other users normally do. For instance, those with lower limbs mobility impairment can move and make gestures inside the Metaverse.

With the help of auto-translation and AI-based captioning, users who are facing language barriers and hearing disabilities can interact with ease. To make them happen, there should be more innovation to factor in the VR hardware.

6. Poised to become a universal virtual destination

Similar to the popular social media platforms today, the Metaverse will be a digital destination where we "hang out and meet." It can be a key factor in determining interpersonal dynamics, relationships, and friendships.

There is no need to travel from one place to another to meet face-to-face. As for marketers and brands, they can harness the advantages of the Metaverse to gain high-traffic advertising.

7. Transform how people live

The advent of the internet has changed the way people live in the past decades. Like the internet, the Metaverse has the potential to transform the personal and professional aspects of our lives.

Its features can be used in anything from socialization, work, gaming, research, development, and so on. Its process-agnostic nature is a key reason why Metaverse is important in the future of digitalization.

Will Metaverse change the way of living in the future?

With the innovations, the Metaverse can change how we interact, shop, work and create value in the real world.

It allows anyone to own a digital property online

There will be vast estates and structures that you can own virtually. These digital assets function as NFT and can be bought through the Metaverse platforms that offer real estate properties.

The Sandbox, Decentraland, and Cryptovoxels are offering plots of land to those who want to invest early in the Metaverse.

It will make the "Play-to-Earn" (P2E) concept more popular

P2E has changed the gaming landscape by offering earning opportunities. This mechanism enhances the fun of building and designing a virtual world. Users spend time creating their own world in the gaming sphere and enjoying the immersive experience of engaging with other players.

Metaverse will enhance these experiences and provide more opportunities for customization and earning while in the game. Decentraland and The Sandbox, both powered by the blockchain are regarded as advanced Metaverse projects.

They are already allowing users to make their own NFTs and sell them to earn cryptocurrency that can be exchanged for fiat currency.

It will create a digital work infrastructure

Metaverse will prevent accidental capturing of employees without trousers while in a remote work setting. It will offer fully-clothed avatars that can be customized.

Horizon Workrooms of Facebook is an early example of a VR-based meeting space that allows colleagues to interact and discuss work-related topics via their individual avatars.

With the digital infrastructure in place, companies can reduce rental payments and enjoy better profits.

It will make online shopping more convenient

Major brands and startup businesses will be competing for consumers' attention with their own Metaverse. Amazon and other major retail businesses are already offering a wide range of products and a quick delivery service but they still lack elements like getting accurate sizes or previewing the item like in real life.

One e-commerce company, the Indian-based Lenskart has already scaled up its services by allowing customers to see how each eyewear frame looks on the face with a video camera. As the Metaverse development progresses, there will be more emerging virtual concepts that offer more convenience to global consumers.

It gives a new meaning to "homeschooling"

When the threat of COVID was scary, schools temporarily closed their doors to prevent the spread of the deadly virus. This forced the administrators of schools to implement "homeschooling" or "distance learning."

To make the virtual setting more conducive and productive, new methods of communication and collaboration were implemented. Some schools even gamified the learning process to make it more interesting to learners.

The emerging digital infrastructure and tech-skilled human resources are important elements in the Metaverse which can eventually influence the concept of learning at home.

It will alter the concept of partying

The coronavirus pandemic made it possible for a lot of companies to be creative. There are new apps that make it easy for party-goers to enjoy online events.

Instagram, Netflix Party, and Houseparty new features have also changed the online partying ideas although they still lack the real-life feel and look. The Metaverse aims to bridge this gap by providing realistic settings.

It can boost tourism and travel via VR tours

When the pandemic hit the tourism industry, some companies reverted to virtual tours. Examples are the popular Greece and Egypt VR tours that allow viewers to visit the beautiful tourist destinations of the lands.

The developers of the Metaverse are planning to make tourist apps that will bring people together, provide information about the spots as well as guide the visitors to achieve the best immersive experiences. In addition, there are plans to re-enact significant events in history, which allows us to cross borders without leaving our homes.

It will bring more exciting adventures

For people who are looking for adrenaline-inducing activities, the Metaverse can power up platforms to allow groups of friends from different locations to go skydiving, racing, or kayaking together.

If you want to travel to outer space but you are not a billionaire like Elon Musk, the Metaverse will make your dream come true. You can even do multiple thrilling activities for a day by accessing different platforms.

It transforms the technology

The Metaverse can change the technology that we will be needing to access and thrive in the digital world. Since this realm is diverse, there is a need to use various applications for seamless operations and functions. Metaverse will change our interactions with computers, making it normal in the future to move our fingers in the air to access our accounts.

At its lowest level, the Metaverse will use built-in cameras just like phones and laptops. Cameras enable mixed-reality mode or display the captured images with the help of an app that is similar to the Pokemon Go interface. As the Metaverse becomes more comprehensive and advanced, there is a need for VR headsets that require high-end smartphones or laptops with a super-fast processor and graphic card.

Potential benefits and drawbacks of Metaverse

The complex design of the Metaverse allows collaboration, communication, workplace innovation, and social interaction within the virtual universe. It comes across as another tech-focused concept that makes us envision and reimagine what the future world will be.

Benefits

1. It opens the door to future "Metawork" or a shared virtual workplace where teams can design, experiment, make changes in the material, or develop blueprints. This secondary environment will redefine who we work with.

2. It allows convenient access to shared content and information.

3. It takes remote working to the next level by allowing full virtual avatars during video conferences. The avatars can interact with colleagues like a real person using different facial expressions and body language.

4. It unlocks new levels of creativity by allowing users to visualize and create solutions in 3 dimensions. It makes it easy to present ideas to clients or make mock-ups of products.

5. It is an infinite space that encourages users to develop new ideas and share them with a lot of people at a given time.

6. It benefits the environment as it significantly lessens waste materials from R & D projects.

Drawbacks

1. It requires excellent technology and maximum bandwidth to enable efficient and fast experiences. Internet penetration is still relatively low in various parts of the globe, except in Northern Europe and North America.

2. It needs a large amount of investment from the Metaverse developers and stakeholders. The high cost of VR gear like headsets, omnidirectional treadmill equipment, and other accessories add weight on the part of the consumers.

   Devices should also be ergonomic and lightweight to make real-world experiences.

3. It needs a mass adoption of remote collaboration. While digital face-to-face has become mainstream when companies and organizations shift to remote work mode, some are not ready to adopt it.

4. It is most likely to raise worries about the protection of shared data and privacy.

Takeaways

- Metaverse has a lot of potentials and benefits, bringing new opportunities for investors and users wherever their location is.

- The decentralized nature of Metaverse and innovative functionalities resolve the typical issues like signing to networks and waiting for authorized permission before we can use the platform.

- The race continues as more major and startup companies join the bandwagon to create a Metaverse.

- The parallel worlds can change how we live in the future as the real world and the virtual world transcends each other to provide functionalities.

- It is best to consider the benefits and drawbacks of Metaverse. It will make us ready to adapt to the transformative innovations that Metaverse can bring.

In the Metaverse, non-fungible tokens (NFTs) or digital assets play a significant role to make the virtual realm more like our physical world. Learn more about NFTs in the next chapter.

Chapter 3

The Role of NFTs in Metaverse

"NFTs are artifacts of networks. So you have your own community and the things, and the NFTs you're creating will be artifacts for that community."- Chris Dixon- American Internet Entrepreneur and Investor

The Metaverse economy greatly depends on non-fungible tokens (NFTs). For the next generation of society, there is a need for digital property authentication to show ownership. The things we purchase in the Metaverse like home, land, clothing, furniture, or vehicle also need to be traded freely between the multiple virtual realms. Another factor that makes NFT important is its capability to be transferred to another owner easily.

NFTs are the digital ownership records that are stored in the blockchain. They enable the robust and decentralized authentication of identities, properties, and possessions. Every single NFT has a corresponding cryptographic key that no one can destroy, copy, or delete.

Currently, it is linked with digital artworks but NFTs' big role in social contracts and independent ownership is enabling the success of the future Metaverse.

Experts in the industry see NFTs as a major value driver of the Metaverse and a transformative economic force of the future. To better understand NFTs' role in the emerging Metaverse, we need to understand this class of digital assets.

> ## Chapter summary
>
> - Non-fungible token (NFT) explained
> - How are NFTs created?
> - Why NFTs have become very popular
> - How do NFTs work?
> - Takeaways

Non-fungible token (NFT) explained

The non-fungible token or NFT came around in 2014 but only gained notoriety recently. During the early days, there were already securitized digital art versions and iconic NBA games video clips on Instagram.

These digital assets were sold online using cryptocurrency and other modes of payment. Since 2017, sold NFTs were valued at $174 million and counting.

Compared to other digital creations with infinite supply available, NFTs have a very limited run. Another thing that sets NFTs different from other digital commodities is their built-in authentication that gives buyers assurance that they are buying original items. Collectors call this proof of ownership the "digital bragging rights."

The most expensive NTF was artist Pak's "Merge". It was sold at a record-breaking $91.8 million. Next was Mike "Beeple" Winklemann's daily drawings called EVERYDAYS: The First 5000 days. The collection was sold at $69.3 million during the auction at Christie's

"Essentially, NFTs create digital scarcity," Yellow Umbrella Ventures managing director Arry Yu said.

NFTs have unique identifying codes similar to cryptocurrencies since they are created using the same underlying software.

However, the likeness ends there. Every NTF comes with a digital signature, making it non-fungible or cannot be exchanged for another. Crypto and physical money are fungible, which means they can be exchanged or traded.

How are NFTs created?

The first-ever NFT was "Quantum." It was created in May 2014 by Kevin McCoy and Anil Dash. The token was a video clip of Jennifer, McCoy's wife. He registered it on the Namecoin blockchain. Dash bought it for $4. The pioneering duo called the NFT technology the "*monetized graphics.*"

The attempt to make a big NFT project occurred in October 2015. The project Etheria was composed of 457 hexagonal tiles which went unsold. In 2017, the awareness about tradable NFTs heightened when the online game CryptoKitties began monetizing their cat NFTs. The market gained traction. After 5 years, the remaining tiles of the Etheria project which were valued at 1 ETH or $0.43 during the launching day were sold out for a whopping $1.4 million.

Another notable example of a non-fungible token is the CryptoPunks, a collection of 10,000 characters that are stored on Ethereum. This project has inspired the CryptoArt movement.

It also shaped the development of the open standard interface or the ERC-721 that powers the majority of the digital collectibles and art. This standard has given the NFT a currency value.

When people believe that Bitcoin and other cryptocurrencies are the digital answer to fiat currency, NFTs become the digital answer to owning rare, valuable collectibles. The unique data of every NFT is easy to verify and validate as the authentic certificate is generated by blockchain technology.

Most NFTs reside on the Ethereum blockchain and exchanges take place in crypto specialist sites. Their value is influenced by the demand for the item and set by the market.

A non-fungible token (NFT) is minted or created from digital objects to represent the intangible and tangible items of real-world items which include:

- Videos and sports highlights

- Digital art

- Music

- Game and related items

- Collectibles

- Video game skins and virtual avatars

- Designer sneakers

- GIFs

- Tweets

- Domain names

- Essays and digital content

Why NFTs have become popular

The resurgence of NFTs around 2017 was due to several factors.

Popularity of cryptocurrency

The exciting things about crypto lie in the framework that combines the laws of scarcity and the economics of royalties. Investors, traders, and consumers want to get hold of the digital currency to leverage its potential. As for the NFT, this digital asset represents ownership of unique digital art or content.

Use of blockchain technology

Ethereum blockchain powers the NFTs in terms of trading, validating, and recording transactions. It eliminates peer-to-peer transactions that reduce the profits of an NFT creator or owner. All products that use Ethereum blockchain share a similar "backend" which makes NFTs portable and easy to sell to other users.

After confirmation of the transaction confirmation, no one can forge or manipulate the ownership data. Finally, Ethereum is stable and secure which means that your NFTs are always up for grabs.

Increased value due to online presence

The more the NFT is seen on social media and other online platforms, the higher value it gains. When it is sold, the current owner of the asset gets 90% of the revenue and the original creator enjoys a 10% share. There is a strong potential for ongoing revenue and increasing value as the assets are traded in the NFT markets.

Unique and distinct value

NFTs are original works, hence authenticity is 100% guaranteed. These digital collectibles have verifiable distinguishing information that is recorded in the blockchain. The record ensures that there will be no fake collectibles to circulate as every NTF can be traced to the issuer or the creator. Moreover, because there are no two NTFs alike, they cannot be exchanged directly.

How do NFTs work?

Technically, NFTs are digital collector's items. They are blockchain-based assets with recorded information in smart contracts. Those who purchase them get a digital file rather than physical forms like actual paintings or CDs. Upon purchase, the buyer gets the exclusive rights to own the file. The unique data of the NFTs makes it convenient to transfer tokens between the rightful owners, validate the ownership, and store certain information. Creators and artists can include their signatures in the metadata of the NFTs.

With NFTs, content creators and artists have found a unique venue to monetize their works. Rather than the traditional way of relying on auction houses or putting their items up in galleries, they can sell them directly to consumers worldwide as NFTs. This means enjoying more profits compared to allowing a third party to sell their creations.

Artists like painters, musicians, composers, and the likes can also program in royalties so whenever their creation is purchased by another owner, they will receive a corresponding sales percentage.

Celebrities are also joining the NFT bandwagon by releasing their unique moments, memories, and artwork.

- Rapper **Snoop Dogg** has an NFT collection "A Journey with the Dogg." It features memories his from early years, Snoop Dogge Coins, an original track entitled NFT, and an NFT-inspired artwork. He launched the collection in a limited 48-hour window and earned more than $100,000.

- Musician **Grimes** released her unique digital artworks and has sold pieces in the amount of $6 million. She is one of the most popular NFT creators., thanks to her bestselling 10-piece WarNymph collection.

- American rapper, record producer, and songwriter **Eminem** raised about $1.8 million in Nifty Gateway when he introduced his collection of NFTs. It included the characters from his videos, digital action figures, and original instrumental tracks.

- **Shawn Mendes** launched his "Wonder" with Genies album in the NFT marketplace OpenSea. According to the Genies CEO Akash Nigam, Mendes earned about $1 million within 10 minutes when the musician offered digital wearables like vests, guitars, earrings, necklaces, and others.

- Socialite, entrepreneur, and Queen of pop culture **Paris Hilton** earned $1.1 million for her Iconic Crypto Queen NFT. She launched her first non-fungible token (NFT) with the vinyl toy and digital collectibles company Super Plastic. Hilton has a collection of about 141 pieces.

- American actress **Lindsay Lohan** introduced her token in Rarible in 2021, which was sold for $50,000. She also released her "Lullaby" single as a non-fungible token on Fansforever, a decentralized social marketplace. It was also reported that she sold for $15,000 the NFT of the defunct EDM duo Daft Punk.

- Supermodel and author **Emily Ratajkowski** purchased back her controversial photograph from Prince to regain control over it. She paid $81,000 to get it back and then photographed herself with the canvas. She created a digital file, launching it as NFT called "Buying Myself Back: A Model for Redistribution." She earned $140,000.

- Artist **Chris Torres**, the man behind the iconic 2011-era Nyan Cat marked the meme's one-decade anniversary by offering a GIF NTF that fetched approximately $600,000. He remastered Nyan Cat by making the original GIF larger and enhancing the minor flaws.

But art is just one way to leverage your income with NFTs. Business brands and sports companies are also navigating this option.

- **Charmin** auctioned off its NFTP or non-fungible toilet paper. The toilet paper-themed NFTs has generated a lot of interest, where bid ranged from $500 up to $2,100. The brand sold five designs, one NFT of each kind. They also came along with a "physical display" if the owners want to hang the NFTP on their bathrooms. The company gives .01% of the sale to Direct Relief, a non-profit humanitarian aid.

- **Taco Bell** NFT art sold out in just a matter of minutes. When the favorite brand tweeted that it would be selling taco-themed images and NFTs on Rarible, the 25 tokens sold out in about 30 minutes. The proceed went to the Live Mas Scholarship, a program supported by the Taco Bell Foundation.

  What makes the NFT cool was the inclusion of a real-world perk of a $500 electronic gift card for the original owner of the non-fungible token.

- **Playboy** launched its Liquid Summer collection of NFTs and sold everything in less than 3 minutes. Its next NFT project "Rabbitars" with unique 11,503 rabbit characters garnered so much attention. Each piece sold at approximately $730.

- **NBA Top Shot** profited from selling NFT memorabilia. It is a collaboration between the National Basketball Association (NBA) and Dapper Labs, the creators of the CryptoKitties game. The collaborative venture has received over $300 million in funding and made more than $230 million in sales.

NBA licenses the content including video reel highlights to the Dapper Labs, which in turn works to digitize the footage. The moments are minted and offered to the marketplace via pack drops. The common packs cost around $9 dollars but the exclusive packs are worth more.

Some of the remarkable video reels that commanded high prices included:

- **Lebron James** NFTs "Cosmic" Dunk ($208,000), "Throwdowns" Dunk ($100,000), "From the Top" Block ($100,000), "Holo MMXX" Dunk ($99,999), and "From the Top" Dunk ($80,000)

- **Zion Williamson** "Holo MMXX" Dunk - $100,000

- **Steph Curry** "Deck the Hoops" Handles -$85,000

- **Giannis Antetokounmpo** "Holoe MMXX" Dunk - $80,000

Crypto art has also grown exponentially with the advent of NFT marketplaces. Collectors look for rare and unique items from the digital markets like Nifty Gateway, SuperRare, and Zora.

Musician Deadmau5 auctioned and sold thousands of collectibles including stickers and digital pins.

Buyers get the privilege of possessing a digital art masterpiece. Each file comes with a license that lets the rightful owner showcase it in his social media pages, personal spaces, virtual museum, or in a digital marketplace (if he plans to resell it).

Takeaways

- NFTs are original, unique assets that are entirely managed through blockchain technology.

- The uniqueness of NFTs' ownership and identity features give them a real value in the world of Metaverse.

With a potential value of Metaverse at $800 billion by 2024, and $10 to $30 billion annual gain in the next 10-15 years, harnessing the power of NFT Metaverse interplay is the key to financial success.

Chapter 4

Blockchain, Cryptocurrency, and NFT Interplay in the Metaverse

"The best way to invest crypto in the Metaverse are by buying NFTs."- Shixing Mao (aka Discus Fish), Co-founder and CEO of COBO

As previously described, **Metaverse** is the virtual world powered by **blockchain** technology where endless possibilities happen. We can build businesses and earn streams of income, create virtual assets, monetize artistic skills, play games, attend or host social events, and a whole lot more.

It is an augmented dimension or reality where we can live an autonomous life. To purchase everything in the virtual world, **cryptocurrency** is needed. The type of crypto depends on the specific Metaverse.

How do blockchain, crypto, and NFTs fit in the Metaverse?

A. Cryptocurrency

Cryptocurrency will be playing a crucial role in the Metaverse. It is the Metaverse's money. Every Metaverse will have its proprietary crypto coin or token that we can use to pay for digital and physical items.

The unique characteristics of crypto serve as a pivotal link that connects the physical and virtual worlds. Cryptocurrencies help us calculate the value of a digital asset in terms of fiat currency as well as the profits and ROIs over time.

It has the key characteristics that cover the aspects of life- digital proof of ownership, accessibility, transfer of value, and governance.

- secure way to show ownership of the virtual items we purchase in the Metaverse
- safe to transfer from one user to another
- right to vote in the decision-making of a Metaverse platform
- liquidity on exchanges that allow investors and traders to sell crypto coins and NFTs to buyers around the world

B. Blockchain

Blockchain has decentralized nature that offers transparency of transactions. Its key elements suit the concept of the Metaverse.

- It provides digital proof of ownership. By purchasing a crypto wallet and cryptocurrency, you become the owner of an asset that is stored in the blockchain.
- It allows the digital collectability of physical items.
- It represents governance through voting rights. Users have the opportunity to control the governing rules and other major activities of the platforms.
- It offers a safe transfer of value anywhere in the world.
- It is more accessible and does not require identity proofs that banks require.

- It is interoperable, allowing seamless interactions and compatibility between multiple platforms for certain projects or activities.

Ethereum blockchain is used by creators as a development platform to create their own Metaverses. ERC20 tokens like SAND (Sandbox) and MANA (Decentraland) are powered the Ethereum to expand their operations or confirm transactions.

In addition, most NFTs can be bought with ETH coins. In essence, Ethereum serves as the driving force for the interconnection of the NFTs, cryptocurrency tokens, and the Metaverse.

C. Non-fungible tokens (NFTs)

Every element in the Metaverse is NFT-**based**, from the smallest item to the largest assets The capability of non-fungible tokens to digitize everything physical and valuable is a significant thing in the development of the Metaverse. This unique capability of NFTs in the birthing of Metaverse explains the growing interest of investors to add digital assets to their financial portfolios.

Once a vague idea that promises great game-changing potential in the art and collectible, the NFT's incredible speed was fascinating when it went mainstream. The common misconception that they are just artifacts or artworks in digital form is replaced by the belief of their potential in the Metaverse.

But before their current popularity, most people outside the crypto space didn't take NFT seriously. Now, celebrities, collectors, and influential people in different industries have embraced non-fungible tokens.

The future of the NFTs will open doors of opportunities for many investors, hobbyists, and entrepreneurs. Industry experts are eyeing NFT's ability to access the Metaverse and define its existence.

The interplay of Metaverse NFT is considered a prominent highlight in the blockchain space. It serves as a key component in the new digital ecosystem. Projects in the Metaverse can be accessed by the use of the NFT. Metaverse's interoperability, versatility, and scalability allow the blending of innovative technologies which include NFTs.

The success of NFTs in blockchain gaming makes it obvious that interoperable games can hasten the Metaverse development. NFTs help in associating real-world identities through the use of digital avatars and in accessing the Metaverse.

With interoperable NFT assets and blockchain as its backbone, the realization of Metaverse spaces is just around the corner in our physical world.

However, there are several hurdles that NFTs need to overcome to ensure successful mass adoption. Moreover, developers of blockchain infrastructure should continue scaling up the use of these digital tokens without compromising the safety of the environment.

There are also things to consider that may happen during the Metaverse development.

- The financial regulators may formulate clear rules on how to deal with digital tokens or NFTs.
- The courts may eventually make case laws regarding NFT copyright disputes if the issue occurs in the future.

Results of Metaverse NFT interaction

To identify the role of NFT in building the Metaverse, it is necessary to understand its capability to change the fundamental design of the concept.

Remember that a non-fungible token (NFT) can initiate disruptions within the conventional social network. It acts as a precedent for users' socialization, interaction, and transaction in the Metaverse.

It makes networking from afar and creating a genuine business without leaving homes virtually possible. The 3D world allows us to port physical assets and services through blockchain technology. This results in the creation of new job opportunities and the emergence of a strong digital economy.

- **It will bring a new generation of identity, community, and social experiences.**

  Users of the Metaverse can express their support for the projects by buying NFT assets. People with the same-minded objectives can form communities to share their experiences or collaborate on content creation.

  In the context of identity, the trending NFT avatars are expected to play a big role in the Metaverse. The avatars become the user's digital representation of the actual self. It can be used to access and switch from one Metaverse location to another.

Think about the NFT avatars as a real-life extension of identities with complete flexibility and control to build digital identities.

With regards to community and social experiences, NFT avatars allow users to become virtual members in the Metaverse and the real world.

- Twitter is supporting NFT profile pictures or avatars, attracting like-minded people to form communities of NFT collectors who buy them for a sense of belongingness, social credit, and status.

- Virtual reality studio House of Kibaa and Gutter Cat Gang's partnership to create animated 3Dd avatars for the creatures in their Metaverse platform. Community members become eligible to win freebies during exclusive raffles like wearables, real estate properties, vehicles, weapons, and pets.

- ## **It will open the road to a transparent and fair economy.**

Metaverse comes with a decentralized environment that opens the possibility of synchronizing interoperable blockchain games with real-world assets. For example, the play-to-earn (P2E) games that offer complete control and ownership of assets to users give an assurance of a fair gaming experience. Using NFTs in the game boosts the chances to earn more and drive Metaverse engagement.

  - Aavegotchhi and Axie Infinity use a pay-to-earn (P2E) model, creating a new virtual economy where players are rewarded with in-game cryptocurrencies and assets like NFTs.
  - Battle Racer releases NFT car parts that users can buy to make or upgrade their vehicles or sell on secondary marketplaces.

Also, the play-to-earn guilds can fuel the rapid growth of the Metaverse NFT interplay since they act as intermediaries to buy in-game lands, assets, and other resources. These gaming guilds give a head start to players who do not have enough capital by lending property and assets.

This empowers the players to earn yields in different Metaverses. The gaming guilds receive a small share of the players' earnings. This approach leverages the power of the NFTs while establishing an open and fair Metaverse economy because anyone can participate and earn.

- reNFT allows users to lend or rent NFTs. The lenders set a maximum period and the daily rate which is an average between 0.002 and 2 WETH (Wrapped Ethereum).

- Several card trading games are offering NFT cards for players to boost the chances of winning. The rental agreement which includes the lease rate and preferred duration is governed by a smart contract.

This fair economy concept is optimized by blockchain's immutability and transparency features. Users of the

Metaverse can also sell their NFT assets like real estate property or in-game collectibles in the marketplaces that support NFTs without any problem.

The possibility of having artificial value inflation is also non-existent. However, the law of demand and supply can still influence the NFT's scarcity and on-chain value.

- ## It will bring new real estate trends.

Metaverse promises virtual spaces with real estate properties. With the help of blockchain technology and NFTs, users can gain ownership of the assets and develop communities by building virtual structures.

Selling Metaverse lands is one of the lucrative NFT Metaverse projects. In the future, NFT holders may have a piece of property in the Metaverse to showcase their own collections or lease it for a profit.

- Lending and renting NFTs to receive passive income. It can be done in the Metaverse through a DeFi (decentralized finance) platform or IQ Protocol of PARSIQ. The IQ Protocol allows virtual real estate owners to generate rent and yield fees from users.

- NFT creators earn royalties when their assets are sold or resold as well as residual dividends. It works when the NFT that represents the asset is used for events like races, events, and activities that require ticket fees or staking.

- **It will level up NFT investing in the Metaverse.**

In 2021, the total spending on non-fungible tokens was over $12.6 billion. Those who have bought profit-generating NFTs, leveraging the optimum potential of their investments.

In the Metaverse, the holders can do a lot more and enjoy more benefits through the following:

- **Yield-generating NFTs** – Investors will enjoy passive returns by supporting Metaverse projects. The holders of the tokens are issued governance tokens that generate residual income.

   Currently, there are collections that are already offering incentives. Genesis Cyber Kongz is planning to make ten $Banana tokens daily for the next ten years. Other examples are the Mutant Cats with $FISH and SupDucks with $VOLT.

- *NFT royalties*. Creators receive a certain percentage of the sales price of their creations whenever they change ownership on the secondary market. The underlying technology that powers the tokens lets the artists set the royalty fee. Once it is predetermined, the smart contracts will automatically enforce the agreements including the distribution of royalty fees.

- *NFT-powered yield farming*. It means leveraging the DeFi protocols to farm for yields using NFT-powered assets. An example of this is using ERC-721 (LP-NFT) tokens from a liquidity provider as collateral or a stake in another income-generating protocol. This allows the NFT owner to earn additional yields.

- **Nested NFTs** – This kind of digital asset offers more intrinsic value to the collectibles. It works by turning the speculative investment into an income-generating asset. Nestled NFTs are layered tokens acting as a digital basket that holds multiple ERC-based tokens. In the Metaverse, they add new functionality and customized features to the digital items.

- **Staking** – Another way to create a passive income from NFT collection is by staking. It means locking up the assets in a decentralized finance or DeFi protocol smart contract in exchange for rewards in form of specific token, voting rights, or governance. Platforms that facilitate non-fungible token staking are Spliterlands, Kira Network, Only1, and NFTX.

- ## It will unlock true asset ownership.

The NFT-powered and blockchain-powered Metaverses offer true ownership of the land, real estate property, digital apparel, avatar, and other items. It allows owners to migrate and use their tokens across different platforms.

It highlights the interoperability feature of the digital asset, unlike the current trend today where users can only utilize their purchased virtual items on one platform or gaming site. The unifying factor can be a single log-in feature or a specific crypto wallet that allows users to access their NFTs.

The non-fungible tokens act as the linchpin of the future economy in the Metaverse. They enable property, identity, and authentication. The cryptographic key of every NFT enables robust security and decentralized verification of the possession. These two factors are important for the Metaverse society to interact with other Metaverses.

What makes NFTs significant is their ability to provide human-like experiences in the real world. They offer an immersive society that resembles a genuine human community. The goods, ideas, and services in digital forms guarantee independent ownership.

"NFTs really started initially with the digital art side. But it's going to be a lot more powerful...so the applications are tremendous," Crypto.com COO Eric Anziani said.

The Metaverse economy and social experience are driven by two elements: *distribution of content* and land ownership. The NFTs enable real estate transactions in the Metaverse using smart contracts.

"For metaverse property rights, you simply cannot fake it because of the way smart contracts are defined, and the NFTs programmed," Anziani added.

The Future of NFT and Metaverse

As the use cases for non-fungible tokens are rapidly expanding, they herald the coming of a new era in the virtual world- the Metaverse. The decision of Facebook to rebrand and launch itself as Meta signaled a shift to the NFT-based augmented reality that will bring the next-gen social networks.

The existing prototype Metaverses in gaming and tech platforms are already giving us glimpses of what will come in the near future. The interconnection of these Metaverses and NFTs in interoperable and blockchain gaming has resulted in million-dollar trading.
NFT gaming is widely popular, where players are spending money to buy cryptocurrency or tokens to upgrade their games.

1. From bringing fun to becoming an investment instrument

The NFTs are like the cool kids in crypto blocks. They represent digital ownership of tangible items. Resurfacing into the mainstream in 2021, this novel concept hit around $25 billion in sales. In 2020, the data of app store DappRadar only showed a $94.9 million sales revenue.

According to personal finance guru Humphrey Yang, *"It's essentially gambling but people don't really know the difference and they buy them because they're fun.*" He believed that buying a non-fungible token is riskier compared to a crypto purchase because it's like betting on virtual currency.

Laura Shin, author and crypto podcast host said that she purchased a music-related NFT out of emotions, not because of investment purposes. "*I bought the Kings of Leon NFT when it came out because I love crypto and I love Kings of Leon.*"

2. Valuable assets that make you part of the exclusive group of owners

Who wouldn't want to be associated with the rich and famous who are in a buying frenzy to get hold of the NFT collectibles?

2021 was a bull run year for Bitcoin and Ethereum. New investors bought shares of this popular crypto and started exploring alternative investments that are crypto-related like Ethereum-based NFTs. All of a sudden, from being a not-so-popular concept since its 2014 inception, this digital asset has become a new medium to monetize original creations and unique memorabilia.

A classic example is the Bored Ape Yacht Club which was offered in a finite number of around 10,000. Stephen Curry purchased one, Jimmy Fallon got one, and Paris Hilton bought one. If you bought one, you are a part of the same group which in a way makes the NFTs more precious from the societal view.

Yang added, *"It's like a membership pass, so the value really comes from other people assigning value to it."*

3. NFTs unbridled evolution through the Metaverse

While some experts believe that NFTs are "bubbles" or "simply a fad", many are claiming that they are here to stay. Laura Shin believed that there will be more NFT mainstream adoption in 2022 and beyond while the Metaverse is slowly building its foundational tech structures. "*They're definitely here to stay."*

It is not the NFT itself that encompasses its strength but the technology behind the tokens. NFTs' real value is defined by the smart contracts on the blockchain, the same innovative technology that empowers and secures cryptocurrency.

Takeaways

- NFTs fit perfectly within the ecosystem of the Metaverse.

- The growing interest of people in non-fungible tokens (NFTs) to access the Metaverse will result in rapid development and expansion of the futuristic platform.

- The opportunity to create a business, trade business, and monetize skills in the Metaverse comes through the NFTs.

- NFTs in the Metaverse represent ownership of acquired original assets and collectible items. They market the properties in the Metaverse.

- Metaverse will boost the popularity of NFTs. On the other side, NFTs will bridge the gap between the digital and physical worlds.

- Blockchain's smart contracts give an advantage to NFTs.

When Blockchain and Crypto meet at the inflection point, the Metaverse will erase

all the doubts that NFTs are just speculative crypto gimmicks. Non-fungible tokens will be part of both virtual and real life. The possibilities will be endless and the next level of the NFT cycle will begin.

Chapter 5

Guide to Metaverse Investing: Will You Be the Next Millionaire

"The phenomenon may be more than a decade away it has the potential to disrupt almost everything in human life."- Jefferies, Investment Banking Firm

The current race to dominate the market is part of the billionaire's battle to dominate the future Metaverse. When Mark Zuckerberg changed the name of the parent company of his social media empire, some people accused him of distracting the attention from Facebook's political furor. Some critics consider him a tech billionaire who is chasing a childhood fantasy like Elon Musk of Tesla and Jeff Bezos of Amazon who is into space rockets.

Yet, his unprecedented move to participate in the development of the Metaverse attracted the interest of investors. It also spiked the price of the platform's stocks by over 9 % which is more than twice that Nasdaq has done. People actively searched Google to understand the terminology and its potential benefits.

Even the notable broker Bernstein predicted that the Metaverse can disrupt major markets with potential $2 trillion annual revenue when the parallel universe materialized. Big tech companies are slowly following in the footsteps of Zuckerberg. No one wants to miss out on the fun and the profits. Even Disney is going in via Disney Metaverse based on the EPIK Prime tweet on November 13, 2021.

Chapter summary

- What will happen to the traditional jobs?
- Available jobs in the Metaverse
- Creative ways to earn money from the Metaverse
- Why is Metaverse considered a lucrative investment?
- How to invest in the Metaverse?
- General steps to start investing in the Metaverse
- What to watch out for
- Takeaways

ArtWallet advisor Dmitry Budorin said that "*Any company building VR/AR technology like Magic Leap, HTC Vive, Varjo, is a metaverse company.*"

He added that companies working to merge the physical and virtual worlds with the help of digital assets like NFTs can be categorized as metaverse developers. It includes those who are creating nootropics products, building biohacking, or doing research on psychedelic topics to alter brain chemistry.

What will happen to the traditional jobs in the Metaverse?

The Metaverse aims to combine all the aspects of life in a single realm. Those who are already working from home can interact with their colleagues in a 3D office. Companies offering traditional jobs can leverage the Metaverse platform for meetings, presentations, and other related tasks.

There will also be Metaverse-related jobs that provide regular income. While the play-to-earn (P2E) gaming models and various online jobs are already giving steady income to people across the globe, the Metaverse can offer more.

Available job types in the Metaverse

- **Digital fashion designers** – They can create designs and experiment with different kinds of materials without actually buying or using them during the presentation or display.

- **Medical professionals** – They can examine the body's digital double to overcome an injury or disease.

- **Smart contract lawyers** – They handle the Metaverse transactions that involve using blockchain technology and new methods to ensure legalities.

- **Metaverse architects** – They work to construct the elements in the Metaverse like an object, place, or experience. This requires expert developers, designers, and creative people.

- **Tour guides** – They are people who will guide new users or visitors around the amazing places found in the Metaverse.

The future of Metawork in the Metaverse is still unknown. However, the current pandemic where we choose between in-house employment and remote work-from-home or a hybrid work system gives us a glimpse of what the future brings.

Creative ways to earn money from the Metaverse

1. Create non-fungible tokens (NFTs)

The Metaverse is opening the doors to all creators who want to monetize their talents and skills. You can turn your creations into digital assets and offer them in multiple marketplaces. Since the Metaverse will be relying heavily on digital items like avatars, collectible cards, equipment, structures, and more, there are a lot of opportunities to sell your original works.

Others can earn a cut from the items that creators make by selling them, becoming a broker, opening an NFT gallery, or advising people about Metaverse.

2. **Run an eCommerce business**

Metaverse is perfect for entrepreneurs who want to open a store in a digital world. It is also easier to kick start a venture virtually than in the physical world where the overhead expenses can be tantamount. Create a shop for your digital products and sell them to your potential customers. Harness the power of social media to advertise your business in the virtual sphere.

3. **Engage in virtual jobs**

The demand for virtual workers such as virtual reality architects, 3D artists, fashion designers, app developers, coders, graphic artists, community managers, and content creators. You can work as a freelancer or work for a company that operates a Metaverse platform.

4. Join the advertising industry

Metaverse will be the next generation social media platform where entrepreneurs and digital creators will be advertising their services and goods. These people will find ways to establish brand awareness and connect with their target audience.

Brands and service companies would be rushing to the Metaverse to make their virtual presence felt. As more entrepreneurs open virtual shops and malls, there will be a massive advertising need. This will turn the Metaverse into a remarkable advertising and marketing place.

5. Design fashion apparel

Expect high-end fashion companies like Gucci and Louis Vuitton to participate in offering virtual clothing NFTs in the Metaverse. You don't need to work for fashion houses to sell your own creations. You can come up with original, creative designs and sell them online.

6. Offer tutorial or mentorship services

You can offer a virtual tutorial or skills enhancement in the Metaverse. If you are a professional artist or mentor, opening an online school is a good idea.

7. Become a travel agent

The Metaverse will have the virtual equivalents of the popular physical destinations, giving rise to jobs in the tourism sector like travel agents and tourist guides.

8. Be a Metaverse product tester

With the popularity of virtual products, there will be jobs for people who can test and provide feedback about them.

9. Host events and promotional campaigns

Entertainment will be a huge part of the Metaverse. You can rent out your virtual properties to host activities or concerts.

10. Promote your social media accounts or YouTube channel

Generate revenue by adding your YouTube channel, Tiktok, or Instagram to the Metaverse platforms.

Why is Metaverse considered a lucrative investment?

The Metaverse is a larger sphere to rake money and opens the door that can create new millionaires. Understand that the crypto investors would also be the "masters" of the virtual platforms. They have dared to invest in digital currencies and reap the profits during the 'bull period.'

Metaverse is believed to deliver gains to investors as it happens. Buying land on the Metaverse platform is the start of lucrative retail opportunities.

Early adopters are adding NTFs and investing in Metaverse projects of giant tech companies. The list of companies that are developing Metaverse-related services and products include Meta (Facebook), Nike (NKE), Roblox (RBLX), Nvidia (NVDA), and Microsoft (MSFT). They offer investment opportunities for those who want to be in the positions when Metaverse eventually unfolds.

Startup entrepreneurs and brand owners know that the Metaverse offers marketing opportunities and direct revenues. This means that there will be more diverse and new kinds of business models and products in the virtual market.

The 3D world of gaming is also rapidly evolving into Metaverses, the alternative online universe where financial transactions happen. Experts believe that the value of Metaverse will continue to rise because of the increasing attention of large tech players.

As the new frontier for digital innovation shapes the landscape, vendors are scrambling to become the pioneering companies to sell the necessary products, apps, and services.

How to invest in the Metaverse

Direct investing

- **Invest in NFTs**

  Investing in the Metaverse through non-fungible tokens (NFTs) is the best option right now. Not everyone can be a tech giant owner who can develop their own metaverse platform. Buy NFT real estate property, in-game assets, and digital art collection. You can also create your own NFTs and sell them in the marketplaces.

- **Invest in Metaverse land and pre-fabricated structures**

  Like crypto investing, buying plots of land in the Metaverse platform is easy. Emerging Metaverse platforms offer more affordable land and structures. You can resell, rent out, or improve your virtual properties to gain more value.

- **Invest in Metaverse projects**

  Invest in crypto-based Metaverse projects that allow you to earn tangible assets and resources. You can exchange the rewards with real-world or digital items. CEO San Morales of the GameFi project believes that *"It's the intersection of gaming and finance."*

Players can earn a living by just winning the challenges in blockchain or online games like the AXS or Axie Infinity. They earn NFTs that can be sold for a fiat currency.

- **Invest in the Metaverse ecosystem**

  Another way is to invest in the foundation builders or the infrastructure-building blockchain projects that ensure interoperability.

  The seamless transfer among different blockchains is a primary element in the Metaverse. Investing in the underlying Metaverse ecosystems and platforms can be lucrative in the long run.

- **Invest in Metaverse tokens.**

  Another way is to invest in social tokens that will be utilized in the metaverse. Tokens are cryptocurrencies made for a brand, community, or influencer.

  These tokens will be an integral part of the metaverse development as new social networking apps will be introduced, resulting in a fandom economy.

Indirect investing

- **Invest in Metaverse-associated stocks.**

    Look for companies that are actively involved in the Metaverse development or producing metaverse products, technologies, and applications.

    The best stocks to invest in at present are Meta (Facebook), Apple, Unity, Cloudflare, Roblox, and NVIDIA. Buy stocks of these companies through Metaverse Exchange Traded Funds (ETF) or brokerages.

- **Invest in MVI (Metaverse Index).**

    The Metaverse index is like a stock market index that captures the trends among the top-performing companies in the gaming, business, and entertainment industries.

    This option is safer than buying Metaverse tokens which are subject to volatility issues. A good example is the Roundhill Ball Metaverse ETF.

- **Invest in secular trends**.

  They represent the potential layers that are necessary to the creation of the Metaverse.

They include Metaverse hardware, 3D creation software, interactive platforms, semiconductor technology, security system, and connectivity.

Basic steps of investing in Metaverse

Step 1: Open an account on your preferred platform.

For crypto tokens, register in a crypto exchange platform to buy them. To buy NFT virtual land or in-game assets, create your account in the proprietary platforms and connect your crypto wallet to store them.

For example, if you want to buy land plots and characters, log on to Axie Infinity. For NFT artworks, register in the Sandbox. If you want to access all types of NFTs in a shared marketplace, OpenSea is your best choice.

Step 2: Create a digital wallet.

Since all transactions within the Metaverse involve virtual currency, you need a crypto wallet to store your purchases.

Step 3: Make a purchase and pay.

Buying is easy. Simply select your preferred token or NFT and pay by using the crypto that you have in your virtual wallet.

Ways to eliminate risks

While there are limitless possibilities of income when you invest in the Metaverse, there are also big risks that could lead to losses if the company fails to meet its goals and expectations. As an investor, you need to choose solid companies that deliver their promises.

For small players, startups, and brand creators, it is crucial to look for vendors who can help in navigating, leveraging, and transforming their businesses.

Here are some tips to consider:

- **Research**

Investing in the Metaverse is far beyond the experience of trying how a new VR headset to enter a virtual space like in gaming. It requires careful research and study of the pros and cons. Researching gives you insights on how to take advantage of the Metaverse and its features.

You can unlock new investment methods or improve digital identity management through blockchain and decentralization. Leveraging its aspects like virtual reality will help you design and build immersive experiences or social communities.

- ## Check the vendor's expertise

Working with the right vendor will help you take your business to the next level. It should help you address specific problems in your niche with the technology you need. The matter of privacy and security that the software or hardware provides is also important.

- ## Be cautious and smart

With Metaverse projects, the price of tokes is relatively low during the early phases of development. It can be 1 cent or less than a dollar, so it is a good opportunity for individual investors to begin investing. But remember that not all projects can give you a good return on investment, so always be cautious.

Avoid putting all your eggs in one investment basket. It is also important that the native token of the platform performs well or has a powerful backup of other investors.

Takeaways

- Understand that Metaverse investing is like any other type of investment that involves winning or losing. It is vital to learn the basics and study the companies offering investment opportunities.

- There several ways to invest in Metaverse- directly or indirectly. Become more familiar with the options before you decide.

- Watch out for the red flags and risks in Metaverse investing. Always follow the investing rules- research, check the background of the company, and never place all your eggs in one basket of investment.

- Know the step-by-step guide to Metaverse investing and how to select the best Metaverse project.

Are you brave enough to invest your hard-earned money to Metaverse? Investing in this tech project is easy and convenient due to its democratic nature. Anyone can buy NFTs, tokens, or crypto assets because there is no minimum entry threshold or geographical barriers.

Chapter 6

Creating Wealth in Metaverse:

Strategy 1-Invest in NFTs

"Any investment is an 'educated gamble' in a market that doesn't even have a universally accepted software platform."- Mike Rhodes, CEO of ConsultMyApp

Metaverse investing offers a great earning opportunity for people in locations that lack capital or do not have stock markets. Expect that more consumer items will be "NFTied" to make them accessible in the Metaverse.

Investing in NFTs that show great potential to increase their value is the key to maximizing the benefits of Metaverse.

The primary reason why people buy NFTs is that they want to start or add incredible pieces of art and other items to their collection. This emerging technology that represents digital content, physical objects, or intangible concepts property is being explored by people for its many uses as well as future profits.

Chapter summary

- Why you should invest in NFTs
- Things to consider when investing in NFTs
- Current and future uses of NFTs
- Guide when buying NFTs
- Where to buy NFTs
- Takeaways

Why you should invest in NFTs

NFT is a new medium that is exciting to explore. These digital assets let you own the sole rights for a recorded sports moment, an artifact, a collectible, or a piece of art. For people who feel the satisfaction of owning a valuable asset, then NFT investing is for you.

But at this point, the merit of the NFTs as a lucrative investment is not yet proven. Their value in the future is highly unpredictable and may cost you some loss. However, their potential to become more valuable has been proven by the celebrities and influencers who enjoyed huge profits when they sold their NFTs.

While some NFTs are worth millions of dollars, there are assets that are not as valuable as them in terms of uniqueness and rarity. One thing is sure, there will be more companies that will enter the business of assets' digitalization and promote their potential applications. Expect that NFTs will become a fixed part of the economy and lifestyle landscapes.

Things to consider when investing in NFTs

If you want to join the growing number of NFTs enthusiasts, consider yourself a collector rather than an investor at this juncture. Investing in NFTs is a matter of personal choice because there are things that hold significant meaning for people.

Bear in mind that the value of NFTs is dependent on the willingness of prospective buyers to pay for them. The demand for the items influences its price and not the economic, technical, or fundamental factors that influence the traditional stocks.

"NFTs are risky because their future is uncertain, and we don't yet have a lot of history to judge their performance," Managing Director Arry Yu of Yellow Umbrella Ventures said.

When buying NFTs, go for the items that make you feel happy and proud to be an owner. Explore the potentials of the assets and have an eye for truly valuable NFTs that may give you a windfall someday. Do your research and consider the risks of every purchase you make. Finally, enjoy hunting down the NFTs you want to acquire but always proceed with caution to avoid losing money down the road.

Take note that NFTs are taxable since they are categorized as collectibles. They are subject to capital gains taxes because they are sold at a profit. The cryptocurrency you use to buy NFTs can also be taxed if it increased in value after the purchase. Talk with a tax professional if you are planning to add non-fungible tokens to your investment portfolio.

Current and future uses of NFTs

- **As digital content**

  Content creators who publicize their works on social media platforms power up the creator economy. As owners of the content, their profit increased when they convert their masterpieces into NFTs.

- **As fashion and wearables digital companions**

  "Collezione Genesis" of Dolce & Gabbana was sold for $5.6 million on September 30, 2021, It was the brand's inaugural 9-piece collection of non-fungible tokens

(NFTs) that is a mix of physical items and digital companions in the blockchain.

Another remarkable event happened at the London Fashion Week when Auroboros unveiled wearable digital apparel with the help of augmented reality (AR). This new brand takes pride in being the first-ever fashion house that merges real-world couture with science and technology.

- **As a cross-platform in the gaming world**

NFTs and online gaming perfectly matched. NTFs offer the gaming developers a new stream of revenue and a way to expand their brands. It allows easier trading of items or characters within the games.

Transactions via the blockchain are fast and convenient, eliminating a middleman who gets a share of your profit. It also opens a lot of possibilities like getting equipment or weapons that are already tested by others.

The advent of Axie Infinity has changed the gaming landscape. By now, gamers do not only play conventional streaming games but also enjoy spending time in the blockchain games. Axie allows participants to cash out their crypto earnings as they exit the game.

This kind of game opens up more possibilities for the Metaverse to boom in the next few years or decades.

CEO of the largest NFT platform OpenSea, Devin Finzer said that *"Gaming is really exciting...have billions of people who are buying digital goods inside of games."* However, he also said that the development cycle is much slower and longer with game stuff compared with collectible and art projects. This restricts the goal of wider adoption. But he was confident that this issue would be resolved soon.

• As investment and collateral

NFTs have a similar infrastructure as DeFi or decentralized finance. DeFi apps allow people to take loans by using collateral. An NFT can be used as collateral to borrow money. For instance, you can take a loan and use CryptoPunk as your collateral.

When you pay your debt, you get your token back. The smart contract will transfer the NFT to the lender directly, eliminating the intervention of a debt collector or a bounty hunter.

NFTs are slowly becoming quasi-securities and are being fractionalized to make them more liquid.

Podcast host and NFT investment company Managing Partner Andrew Steinwold said *"NFTs enable some new behaviors of assets."* Sfermion is an NFT investment company.

- **As eternal web domain names**

  NFTs can make your domain more valuable and memorable. It works by making the IP address easier to recall based on the relevance and length of the name you choose. A simple and easy-to-remember URL makes a big difference in the website's marketing goals. This is why some domain names are very expensive.

  There are also people who wait for the expiration of the popular domain names and engage in *'domain sniping'* or buying it immediately.

  To avoid a similar thing from happening, opting for an NFT domain name is the best solution. *Unstoppable Domains* headed by Matthew Gould said that they are offering blockchain-based domain names. You can purchase an available domain name and register it as a non-fungible token and store it in a crypto wallet. Users only need to pay a one-time fee for the domain, rather than the periodic fees that traditional domain name registrars require.

With an NFT domain name, the ownership is perpetual and cannot be snatched by opportunists.

- ## As an authenticity indicator

Checking the authenticity and rarity of a product or investment asset is assured by the NFTs. They can store everything including the manufacturing process to prove fair trade and transparency.

In the long run, NFTs are considered the answer to the proliferation of fake products, medicines, and supplements as vital information can be tracked down easily from manufacturing to shipment processes.

- ## As an enabler of fast and hassle-free real estate transactions

Real estate NFTs are perfect for each other. NFTs can be used to enable smart contracts that allow auto-payment schemes, track down fresh updates of property values, provide proof of ownership, create decentralized rental services, transfer land deeds, and protect sensitive data of clients like information on their credit cards.

In the real world, the land is finite. It is one thing that no one can make more of. But the virtual worlds like The Sandbox, Decentraland, and Cryptovoxels are leveraging this element to make their platforms more popular. It is something that the Metaverse world can offer.

Owning digital real estate allows us to create a virtual community and build buildings. We can offer spaces for retail merchants, startup firms, or organizations that want to host a virtual event. The possibilities are endless.

- **As protector of patents and intellectual property**

NFTs give users the authority to prove their ownership of any content, unlike the copyrights, trademarks, and other traditional IP rights tools. The timestamps offer transparency and accessibility of the whole IP history and distinguishable elements.

For patent purposes, NFTs can certify and protect the invention or innovation ownership by providing the necessary verification data. All patent-related matters are documented in the public ledger or blockchain.

• As verifier of medical records

Ledgers of non-fungible tokens can store the medical records of patients and keep them protected since all transactions are validated by multiple nodes. This prevents the risk of tampering and compromising the confidentiality of information. Every record is verified true and correct before it is added permanently to the blockchain.

Retrieving the stored sensitive data is easier for the authorized medical providers, helping hospitals and health insurance firms to access the data.

NFTs applications are also specifically designed for healthcare professionals to issue NFT birth certificates. The identities of newborns are stored on the blockchain and are linked to verified birth certificates

• As digital identity proof

One of the intriguing apps in the blockchain is the SSID (self-sovereign identity). It is a decentralized feature of this technology, allowing users to entirely own their names in the digital community. SSID has the power to re-democratize the future of the internet where every post, article, video, picture, or tweet has a cryptographic signature that verifies the identity of the author.

By creating an NFT of identity, it would be easier to link all social media accounts and online platforms. It would exist as proof of our digital identity. Owning our identity is like having a digital passport that proves our existence.

An NFT identifier is not controlled by any authority like the government or a third party like Facebook or YouTube. We are the sole custodians of our data and we control what we choose to share. We may even license or sell the valuable data we possess.

- **As a representation of academic credentials**

  NFTs can provide important academic information including degree earned, proof of school attendance, the record of achievements, and other pertinent data.

  All information recorded on the NFT chain can be transferred to the requesting party without the usual paper certificate. Issued NFTs can be verified through the verification system of smart contracts.

- ## As a tracking partner of the supply chain

NFTs offer manufacturing and distributing companies the capability to keep track of their products. The food industry will be benefitting a lot because NFTs help in verifying the ingredients, where they come from, and other factors.

With the attached NFT identifier, it would be easier for customers to know if they are spending money on a good product. In addition, it sustains transparency within the supply chain of the company.

- ## As a lost artwork tracker

NFTs allow physical art to become digital and physical art can be created into digital tokens. For original artworks, converting them into NFTs help to track counterfeits or stolen ones. This helps in eradicating or reducing the number of counterfeits as well as tracking the originality of the pieces that people bought from auction houses.

- ## As a ticketing option

In the future, there is a big chance that NFTs will replace the traditional tickets or passes with a unique ID that allows access to restricted areas. It reduces paper usage and fraud issues because the NFT owners need a single token for everything that is related to the purpose.

For instance, if you are attending a musical concert, the NFT pass that you purchased would give you the following benefits:

- access to the event or location

- exclusive pass to digital goodies

- memorabilia of the event

- means to get free snacks

- makes you a shareholder of the event if the NFT is offered as event equity (you get a cut of the profit)

NFT-minting platform Mintbase's co-founder Carolin Wend said *"What excites us is NFTs being used in the real world."*

An example of this was the Mintbase's NEARCon Festival in Lisbon on October 26, 2021, which used the smart contracts system NEARProtocol. The organizers of the festival decided to do a hundred percent NFT ticketing, allowing attendees to stake the tickets or earn a certain profit.

- **As a voting document**

  Voters are required to show an ID or a document that shows proof of residence before casting their votes. NFTs can be used to integrate people's identities and store sensitive data like who they voted for. Moreover, NFTs may help a lot to prevent voter fraud and cheating issues.

Guide when buying NFTs

Before you get hold of these specialized tokens, here are the things you need to prepare to buy them:

1. Digital Wallet – It stores your cryptocurrencies and acquired NFTs.

2. Cryptocurrency – You need to buy the crypto that the NFT providers accept as payment for the digital asset. Ether is mostly accepted by sellers.

3. Crypto exchange- Find secure platforms that sell cryptocurrencies like Coinbase, PayPal, Kraken, and OpenSea.

Where to buy NFTs

Since the breakthrough of the NFTs in the virtual market, there are many marketplaces that emerge. There are categorized in terms of subject nature, format, style, and collection. Generally, the four types are the following:

- Open marketplace. It has a wide array of digital assets and art from various sources and creators.

- Collectible marketplace. It is focused on movies, sports, or art collectibles.

- Curated marketplace. Its NFT selection comes from specialized or specific sources.

- Games marketplace. It offers game-related NFTs.

Top NFT marketplaces to check out:

OpenSea

OpenSea is the largest non-fungible token marketplace. It is considered the 'eBay" of digitalized assets with a wide array of art, photos, sports memorabilia, music, and more. This platform supports creators of all types and accepts over 150 payment tokens. It is also one of the best sites for minting new tokens.

You need to create your account on the website before you can browse and buy the available collection of non-fungible tokens. OpenSea is known for offering rare pieces of collectibles and digital items.

Rarible

Rarible is a community-driven marketplace with minting capabilities of creators' NFTs and portfolios. It allows artists and creators to offer their digital assets and collectibles. It also provides royalties to the creators for the future sales of their minted assets. You can find major brands in this marketplace like Adobe and Taco Bell. It requires Rarible tokens as payment.

Foundation

Foundation is launched in 2021. It is one of the high-end marketplaces for digital art. It is an exclusive community where artists need an invitation from their co-artists and creators before they can post their art. This artist-curated platform has sold over $100 million worth of NFTs. To purchase, users need a crypto wallet with Ethereum coins.

Mintable

Mintable is an open marketplace that supports the NFT minting needs of all kinds of creators and artists. It is viewed as the "Etsy" of the digital asset marketplace. Billionaire Mark Cuban backs up this platform.

Known Origin

Known Origin is like a real-world art gallery as it caters to the NFTs of the photographers and artists. It offers the most expensive collections.

SuperRare

SuperRare is another higher-end NFT marketplace. It has an art gallery vibe and is more selective. It offers 3D images, videos, and art. It recently launched its own token for buying and selling purposes.

Nifty Gateway

Nifty Gateway is another curated platform for artists. It is powered by the Gemini crypto exchange. Its NFTs are created on Ethereum and are called "Nifties". This site also hosts non-fungible tokens for buyers who prefer a third party to store the items for them. You can view and buy many celebrity NFTs here. It facilitated the bestselling sale of Beeple and other digital creators.

DraftKings Marketplace

DraftKings Marketplace is a sports-themed site that offers collectible artifacts of popular names like race car drivers, football stars, and hockey stars. It is built on the brand's existing franchise of sports betting platforms.

NBA Top Shot

NBA Top Shot is the NFTs marketplace for basketball fans. It has the best selection of play highlights and video clips that captured historic games. It is NBA-authorized and does not offer a minting option for creators. What you see is what you get on this platform.

The price of collectibles varies from a few dollars to thousands. It is now a billion-dollar marketplace of NFTs after its substantial success.

Axie Infinity Market

Axie Infinity Market is a gaming NFT site where assets of the popular game can be sold, bought, and minted. It is instrumental to the success of Axie in the gaming ecosystem and has over a billion dollars in market cap. Its proprietary tokens, Axie Shards can be purchased from crypto exchanges and other NFT marketplaces.

Other places to buy NFTs are Binance NFT, Decentraland, Arkane Market, Async Art, Ether cards, BakerySwap, Ghost Market, Makers Place, Larvalabs, Theta Drops, NFT Showroom, Zora, Treasureland, and Viv3.

Takeaways

- If you know what kind of NFT asset you want, you can go ahead and check the specific marketplace. However, the challenge is determining which among the several sites offers the best deal. It is important that the marketplace has the right NFTs for you and its reputation in the NFT world.

Find answers to the following questions:

- o What are the existing safeguards that ensure legitimate and safe transactions?

- o What are the available NFTs? Are there similar options?

- o What are the transaction fees involved?

- o What is the required cryptocurrency to buy an NFT?

- o Where to store the purchased NFT?

- o Where and how to re-sell the NFTs? Does it help in reselling the item when you decide to?

One of the easy ways to invest in Metaverse is to purchase the proprietary token of the platform. All you need is a

fiat currency, a digital wallet, and an account in a crypto exchange platform or the Metaverse platform. Check out the top Metaverse tokens that are creating a big buzz today.

Chapter 7

Creating Wealth in Metaverse:

Strategy 2-Buy Metaverse Tokens

"The key to a successful metaverse token is its utility."- John Dough, Crypto Analyst of Currency.com

Cryptocurrency has become mainstream, thanks to the staying power of Bitcoin. Ethereum and other altcoins showed positive performance too in 2021. And because of this growing interest in virtual currency, many investors are on the lookout for new opportunities to grow their financial portfolios.

When NFTs or non-fungible tokens within virtual games become popular, the online marketplaces began offering digitalized artworks and collectibles. The venture proved to be lucrative and created another avenue of income.

Then comes the metaverse tokens. They are the evolution of cryptocurrencies. They are created using blockchain technology, making them generally secure like the first generation of crypto coins.

Chapter summary

- A walkthrough of the best Metaverse tokens
- Types of Metaverse tokens
- Why is it important to consider the market cap of the Metaverse tokens?
- Top-performing Metaverse coins by market cap (in billions)
- Takeaways

A walkthrough of the best Metaverse tokens

Every Metaverse platform has its own cryptocurrency, whether it is a gaming, social, real-estate, or e-commerce platform. In essence, the metaverse tokens are the currency in the 3D platforms. They are the money that is used to pay for assets in the Metaverse or to create digital products or services.

With digital currencies, any user can buy in-game accessories, items, and upgrades, buy or sell virtual lands, and other NFTs. Some tokens are only available in the respective Metaverses, while most of them can be purchased on crypto exchanges and NFT marketplaces.

Types of Metaverse tokens

- **Play-to-earn (P2E) coins**

  P2E coins are in-game currencies with a real-world value that can be exchanged for fiat currencies. When players engage and win the challenges in the game, they receive rewards in the form of metaverse tokens.

- **Metaverse platforms coins.**

  They are the utility tokens of the Metaverse platforms or the blockchain's cryptographic assets with unique metadata and identification codes.

- **3D digital metaverse coins**

  They are generally referred to as non-fungible tokens (NFTs) used for commercial transactions in the Metaverse. The 3D platforms provide virtual experiences which include e-commerce and P2E gaming. To access them, users need the proprietary tokens.

Why is it important to consider the market cap of the Metaverse tokens?

The market cap measures the value of the cryptocurrency. It provides the crypto coin or token's detailed overview, allowing investors to compare its value against other cryptocurrencies. It also helps in determining the coin's volatility and potential growth. To find out the market cap, simply multiply the total number of mined coins by the single coin's current price in the market.

To demonstrate:

- Crypto X has 500,000 coins in circulation. Each token is valued at $1. The **market cap** of Crypto X is $500,000.

- Crypto Z has 200,000 coins in circulation. Each coin is valued at $2. The **market cap** of Crypto Z is $400,000.

Like the conventional investment, it is important to consider the market cap or the total dollar value of mined coins.

The larger the coin's market cap, the greater the stability that it offers to investors. Crypto coins with smaller market cap are susceptible to the constant changes in the market, creating dramatic gains or losses.

Generally, there are three types of market capitalization – large-cap (companies with $10 billion or more), middle or mid-cap (with $2 to $10 billion), and small-cap (with $300 million to $2 billion).

- The **large-cap** companies are the major players in the industry and have been around for a longer time.

  While they do not necessarily guarantee huge returns within a short-term investment period, the longer-term investment rewards their investors.

- The **mid-cap** companies are those showing a rapid growth in the industry. Their potentials are great and can give a good return on investment.

- The **small-cap** companies are younger in the industries or serving a niche market. Typically, they have fewer resources and are vulnerable to economic slowdowns.

1. ApeCoin

The token

ApeCoin is a governance and utility token of the APE Ecosystem. This ERC-20 token empowers and incentivizes the builders of Web3 in the decentralized metaverse. It is an ERC-20 token that is secured by the proof-of-work (POW) consensus mechanism of the Ethereum blockchain.

The total supply of this token is fixed at 1 billion and is all minted. During the launching on March 17, 2022, about 30.25% of them were circulated. Every 48 months, this percentage will increase to allow investors to buy and trade them.

The platform

APE was inspired by the Bored Ape Yacht Club Project of the Yuga Lab. This decentralized project is supported by the APE Foundation to maintain an inclusive, fair ecosystem that allows open, permission-less collaboration in governance. The proposals of the APE Foundation are approved by the members of the community. Holders of APE can vote on how the ApeCoin DAO Ecosystem Fund is utilized.

2. MANA

The token

Ethereum-based **MANA** is the native token of Decentraland. It held the record of being the first metaverse crypto, giving it the time to establish authority in the market. Holders of this token can buy parcels of lands and in-game items in the form of NFTs. The token also provides the right to participate in the governance of the platform and influence the changes in the game itself.

When it was launched in 2018, one MANA was at $0.025. It jumped from less than $1 in October to $5.90 in November, gaining an overall 4,000% growth at the end of 2021 after successfully attracting high-profile investors. According to CoinMarketCap, investors who purchase tokens in 2017 would enjoy up to 12,000% ROI if they choose to sell their MANA. It is one of the best metaverse tokens to invest in.

MANA Value Statistics (*subject to change*)

1 MANA – $1.86

1 MANA – 0.00004852 Bitcoin

1 MANA – 0.0006644 ETH

Market Capitalization - **$3.4 billion**

Fully diluted market cap - $ 4.0 billion

Circulating Supply – 1.84 billion MANA

The platform

Decentraland is powered by the Ethereum blockchain. It is a leading virtual reality platform with over 300,000 users monthly who can freely access the 3D world by browsing. With over 90,000 plots that are represented by NFTs, Decentraland is a leading metaverse project that allows users to create, experience, and monetize their content.

Its decentralized nature supports the social aspect of the growing user base. The active ecosystem of this platform is composed of businesses and individuals who enjoy creating communities, structures, space adventures, and scenes.

- The most notable was when the **Government of Barbados** opened its metaverse embassy on the platform, becoming the first country to invest in the virtual world.

- It was followed by **The Metaverse Group**, a subsidiary of Tokens.com purchased Decentraland's most expensive space for $2.4 million for their e-commerce businesses and digital fashion shows.

- Other big names inside the Decentraland are Samsung and JPMorgan Chase. The cheapest plot of land in Decentraland is around 2.88 Ether ($8,500).

3. SAND

The token

The Sandbox's native token is the ERC-20 **SAND** that can be used to participate in a play-to-earn (P2E) game, purchase digital items, and create your own non-fungible tokens (NFTs). You can sell the NFTs in the marketplace or integrate them into the game with the help of the Game Maker.

SAND is used to pay for ASSETS (or NFTs), equipment to power up the gameplay, avatars, or game access. Players also earn SAND as a reward by playing the game. All transactions in the platform use this token including staking to earn interest.

This native virtual currency was first listed in mid-2020 on public exchanges at $0.051. In November 2021, the value of SAND reached another all-time high of $8.44. In 2021, its value has grown by 16,000%. During the same period, The Sandbox has also sold more than $144 million worth of merchandise. Investors who bought SAND during the launching could expect up to a 4,000% return if they will sell them today.

The platform

The Sandbox is another popular Metaverse project that is utilizing VR technology. This virtual game allows users to create their own experiences, content, or game and monetize them.

Built on the revolutionary Ethereum blockchain, it allows users to build and design buildings, clothing, characters, or vehicles.

To do anything in the platform, users need its proprietary crypto SAND. All items that are created by participants are added to the public ledger or blockchain in NFT form. They can be sold and bought. The Sandbox also incentivizes users who stake to earn interest or invest in SAND.

This project was launched in 2012 and eventually expanded its business model and focused on the Metaverse development. The Sandbox is aiming to become a DAO (decentralized autonomous organization) by 2023, hence it has allocated a huge portion of the circulating token to the investors and team members. Notable brands that partnered with The Sandbox are Adidas and SoftBank Vision Fund 2.

4. THETA

The token

THETA is the native token of Theta Network, the first video streaming dApp (decentralized application). It is used for staking validator, governance, or guardian node. This crypto token was created in January 2021 to empower the network's goal of becoming the leading media and entertainment blockchain infrastructure company.

The market value of THETA reached an all-time high during the crypto boom in 2021, from $1.86 in January to $15.90 in April.

It ended at $4.71 in December with a 153% gain in 2021. The top crypto exchanges where you can trade these tokens are Binance, Upbit, DigiFinex, OKX, and Kucoin.

> **THETA Value Statistics** (*subject to change*)
>
> 1 THETA – $2.80
>
> 1 THETA– 0.00007287 Bitcoin
>
> 1 THETA – 0.0009971 ETH
>
> Market Capitalization - **$2.8 billion**
>
> Fully diluted market cap - $ 2.8 billion
>
> Circulating Supply – 1 billion THETA

The platform

With its own blockchain, the **Theta Network** is able to offer economic and technical solutions to streaming problems. The crypto-video delivery ecosystem of the Theta network incentivizes bandwidth sharing where users can share their excess computing resources and bandwidth in return for tokens. This greatly improved the quality of stream delivery and reduced the cost.

It has successfully expanded its traditional computing, data delivery, and video products by adding decentralized storage of NFTs and other digital items.

- Singer Katy Perry launched her first-ever NFT collections in December 2021 after acquiring a stake in the network's developer Theta Labs.

- Theta Network has forged a partnership with NASA and ONE Championship.

- Its ecosystem is backed up by SAMSUNG NEXT, Sonny Innovation Fund, and other big corporations.

5. XTZ

The token

XTZ is Tezos utility token. The market price of XTZ spiked to $9.18 on October 4, 2021, when the open-source blockchain Tezos did an upgrade.

It reached another all-time high in December when Ubisoft entered the NFT market via Tezos.

XTZ Value Statistics (*subject to change*)

1 XTZ – $2.82

1 XTZ– 0.00007345 Bitcoin

1 SAND – 0.001004 ETH

Market Capitalization - **$2.5 billion**

Fully diluted market cap - $ 2.5 billion

The platform

Tezos is a smart contract platform was founded by couple Arthur and Kathleen Breitman in 201. It is designed to be decentralized at all levels, allowing the token holders to vote for the proposals of the administrator of Tezos. The stakeholders can also propose, evaluate, and approve changes to the network upgrades. With modular architecture, the system's components can be linked together.

Tezos is focused on three main elements:

- Safety of smart contracts

- Open participation

- Long-term upgradability

6. AXS

The token

AXS or **Axie Infinity Shard** powers the Axie Infinity platform. This NFT-based token is one of the popular metaverse cryptocurrencies. It is used to buy, breed, or trade NFT pets called Axies. It also serves as a governance token that allows holders to vote on the platform's continuing development. Staking AXS gives players weekly rewards. The tokens can be converted into real-world fiat currencies. AXS can be traded on top crypto exchanges like Coinbase, Binance, Kraken, Bithumb, Huobi Global, Upbit, OKX, DigiFinix, KuCoin, FTX, and Gate.io.

When AXS was launched in the early part of 2020, it was priced at $0.15 per token. It peaked on November 6, 2021, at $165.37, translating to 110,000% growth. A single in-game transaction can cost users $420. At the end of 2021, a virtual land in Axie Infinity was sold for $2.5 million.

Value Statistics (*subject to change*)

1 AXS – $40.65

1 AXS – 0.00105 Bitcoin

1 AXS – 0.01443 ETH

Market Capitalization - $**2.4 billion**

Fully diluted market cap - $ 10.9 billion

Circulating Supply – 60.9 million AXS

The platform

Axie Infinity is a top-performing P2E, Pokemon-inspired game that is close to the essence of the metaverse. It is averaging over 1 million daily players. This NFT crypto-gaming pioneer was founded by Sky Mavis in 2018 and developed on the Ethereum-based Ronin Sidechain.

Its native token AXS is one of the popular metaverse tokens that can be purchased from top crypto exchanges. Users can also earn it by playing games and participating in various campaign challenges on the platform.

Axie Infinity has another cryptocurrency- the smooth love potion or SLP that is utilized to breed new Axies. It is awarded to users who spend time playing on the platform.

This metaverse project is continuously upgrading its features which boosts the sales of AXS. It has also introduced staking, allowing traders to earn incentives when they invest in.

7. GALA

The token

GALA is the utility token of the platform. The creators of this metaverse crypto designed it to support blockchain-powered gaming ecosystem by providing a futuristic and immersive experiences. It is used as in-game rewards, node operator incentives, network governance, peer-to-peer payments, and buying NFTs from the Gala store. Users can run a Gala Node from their home if they have the necessary equipment. As incentives, they can earn free GALA and rare NFTs.

Since its launching, the network has sold more than 26,000 NFTs. The most expensive was about $3 million. There will be 35 billion GALA tokens to be minted.

About 7 million are circulating at present and half of it is distributed to the operators of Founder's Nodes or the PoWs, representing the first supporters of the platform. You can purchase GALA tokens from Uniswap V3, Sushiswap, KuCoin, Gate.io, and Bitrue.

GALA Value Statistics (*subject to change*)

1 GALA– $0.1721

1 GALA– 0.000004488 BTC

1 GALA – 0.00006135 ETH

Market Capitalization - **$1.2 billion**

Fully diluted market cap - $ 6.1 billion

Circulating Supply – 6.9 billion GALA

The platform

Gala is a Metaverse gaming platform powered by blockchain technology. It has high-quality, engaging games that are fun to play with like RPG games, PvP tower defense games, and MOBA. Within the ecosystem of the game, users can buy in-game items in NFT form with the native token GALA.

It was founded on July 21, 2019 by Eric Schiermeyer who was a co-founder of Zynga company that distributed the popular mobile and social games Farmville, Mafia Wars, and Poker.

With an aim to create a gaming ecosystem where players can own and trade in-game assets or NFTs, Schiermeyer made another cutting-edge opportunity for global users to take back their control. This is to eliminate the issue of losing all the assets or achievements with accidental clicking of the button.

8. ENJ

ENJ is the local currency of Enjin Coin, an NFT marketplace that aims to offer advanced digital economies via blockchain technology. This coin directly correlates with the NFT value in the platform, making it the gold standard for virtual assets.

ENJ is also a limited resource that backs NFTs, making it more valuable in regulating asset creation and preventing inflation.

In order to make build items in the game ecosystem or create NFTs, users need to utilize

ENJ and infused them into digital assets. ENJ tokens have unlimited capacity, allowing the participants to use the purchased NFTs in multiple games. The more games the platform provides, the more these metaverse tokens will be popular and command a higher price.

Moreover, holders can melt the NFTs into ENJ whenever they want. Through this process, the value of the digital assets escalates because of the principle of scarcity. It results in boosting the confidence of investors in the projects and blockchain assets that are powered by the Enjin Coin.

ENJ Value Statistics (*subject to change*)

1 ENJ– $1.29

1 ENJ– 0.00003358 Bitcoin

1 ENJ – 0.0004596 ETH

Market Capitalization - **$1.1 billion**

Fully diluted market cap - $ 1.2 billion

Circulating Supply – 881.9 million ENJ

The platform

Enjin Coin was founded in 2009 by Witek Radomski and Maxim Blagov. It is a gaming community platform. Radomski was the author of one of the first NFTs and the author of Ethereum token standard ERC-1155.

This Metaverse project features an NFT trading marketplace, crypto wallet, and a platform that lets developers create their own apps or games. To create NFTs or build items in the ecosystem, the token ENJ is used.

All in-game items are interconnected and run on the platform, letting the participants use their purchased products in different games.

Its ecosystem allows all sizes of businesses and game developers to utilize tokenized assets for engagement, monetization, acquisition, or retention purposes. It utilizes smart contracts to allow the game developers to mint new non-fungible ERC-1155 tokens.

Takeaways

- The native token of the platform fuels the functionalities of the Metaverse. It is the currency that makes the operation runs smoothly and becomes successful.

- Know the different types of Metaverse tokens – P2E coins, platform utility coins, and NFTs.

- Before buying Metaverse coins to harness the power of the platform, consider their market caps to ensure the platform's financial stability.

- Check out the top-performing Metaverse coins with billions of dollars in market capitalization.

Another way to leverage the power of the Metaverse is to invest in platforms that are now on the road to harnessing its potential. Find out in the next chapter the best platforms to invest your money and the companies behind them.

Chapter 8

Creating Wealth in Metaverse:

Strategy 3-Invest in Metaverse Platforms

"The Metaverse has become the newest macro-goal for many of the world's giants."- Matthew Ball

When Facebook rebranded and became Meta, there is a sudden interest in the alternate world known as the Metaverse. The thought of sitting on your couch while doing a regular day job, interacting with colleagues, or shopping in other parts of the globe is not a far-fetched dream anymore.

Currently, numerous tech and non-tech companies that already set the motion to upgrade their platforms and embrace the coming of the full Metaverse. Projects that are related to Metaverse seem to be the trend of the moment, causing the industry players to join the race so they will not be left behind.

Chapter summary

- What makes a game-focused Metaverse project viable?
- Elements of a good Metaverse project
- 20 best platforms to consider this 2022
- Takeaways

Those in the gaming industry are the first ones to decide in upgrading their technology, applications, and infrastructure. As early as now, they are already trying to outdo one another to dominate the early stage of the Metaverse and boost their user base.

What makes a game-focused Metaverse project viable?

✓ Its Metaverse is developed around the primary game.
✓ It shows a strong partnership with A-list industry investors.
✓ It has a play-to-earn (P2E) mechanics.
✓ It has partially or fully-launched game features.

- ✓ It has an active community on its social media channels.
- ✓ It has frequent media coverage and displays prominence in the market.
- ✓ It features advanced gameplay and graphics.
- ✓ It is IDO-completed with available tokens for trading
- ✓ It has a fully detailed roadmap and whitepaper
- ✓ It has completed significant presale and funding rounds.
- ✓ It delivers regular project development progress reports.
- ✓ It has low rug pull risks.

Elements of a good Metaverse project

There are many Metaverse projects in the marketplace now. As an investor, it is crucial to have a checklist of criteria to ensure that you are doing the right choice.

- ✓ It offers a wide range of immersive experiences (gaming, social, commerce)
- ✓ It has an advanced 3D ecosystem.
- ✓ It has active social media channels and communities.
- ✓ It displays a strong market prominence.

✓ It receives good reviews and has frequent media coverage.
✓ It has multiple partnerships with well-known industry investors.
✓ It has a fully detailed whitepaper and roadmap.
✓ It is IDO-completed with an available native crypto token.
✓ It has completed presale and funding rounds.
✓ It offers regular updates on the progress of the metaverse development.
✓ It has partially launched features with upcoming or ongoing alpha testing
✓ It has minimal risks.

So, which are the best Metaverse platforms to choose when eyeing potential gains aside from the ones listed in the previous chapter? Let's explore the performance, features, and highlights of the following platforms.

Best platforms to consider this 2022

1. WAX

The platform

WAX is a decentralized app with blockchain-based tools that went public in 2017. The suite of tools allows the creation of non-fungible tokens (NFTs) and DApp marketplaces.

The network operates on the DPoS (delegated proof of stake) consensus mechanism. Behind this company are Jonathan Yantis and William Quigley who aim to provide users of safer and faster e-commerce transactions.

The token

WAXP is the token of WAX, which can be converted into WAXE (the ERC-20 utility token) of the platform. Participants of tokenomics have to burn their WAXP to get hold of WAXE.

The WAXE tokens are utilized for staking. With these tokens, the users gain WAXG (governance token of the network) and enjoy the right to vote on proposals. WAXP is available in Binance, Bithumb, Bitfines, Crypto.com, HitBTC, and Huobi Global.

WAXP Value Statistics (*subject to change*)

1 WAXP– $0.2678

1 WAXP– 0.000006538 Bitcoin

1 WAXP – 0.00008732 ETH

Market Capitalization - **$ 528.1 million**

Fully diluted market cap - $ 1 billion

Circulating Supply – 1.97 billion WAXP

2. Ontology

The platform

Ontology is a China-based metaverse project that was launched in 2017. It was founded by Li Jun with the objective of creating an infrastructure that offers secure access to Web 3.0. This low-cost, high-speed public blockchain can facilitate up to 4,000 transactions in a second and in certain test environments can reach 12,000 transactions.

In terms of hosting ability, experts in the industry believe that it can be one of the best blockchain networks. It provides flexibility to businesses when creating their own blockchain, allowing them to customize it to match their objectives and needs. It is fully decentralized and highly resistant to hacking issues.

The token

The native token of Ontology is **ONT**. It has a total supply of 1 billion units and is available in Binance, Crypto.com Exchange, BingX, OKX, and DigiFinex.

3. Radio Caca

The platform

Radio Caca is created by the Universal Metaverse or USM Lab, a 3D gaming world where players can own plots of land, make buildings, play or create their games. It is operated by the decentralized association (DAO) that is composed of internet-native people across the world whose ultimate goal is to build a metaverse. This company acts as the exclusive manager of the NFT "Maye Musk Mystery Box."

The token

RACA is the native currency of Radio Caca It is used by players to create their own games, buy and cultivate lands, build structures, travel on the virtual planet, and more. It is the ideal metaverse token for creating NFTs. It can be purchased and traded in OKX, Bitget, Phemes, Bybit, and DigiFinex.

RACA Value Statistics (*subject to change*)

1 RACA– $0.001442

1 RACA– 0.0000000447 Bitcoin

1 RACA – 0.0000006087 ETH

Market Capitalization - **$ 446.8 million**

Fully diluted market cap - $ 720.8 million

Circulating Supply – 309.8 billion RACA

4 . WEMIX

The platform

With over 600 million active users, **WEMIX** is a GameFi platform that powers various games like Mir 4. Its blockchain ecosystem also provides DApps with infrastructure to operate seamlessly, eliminating the low transaction speed or high gas fees. The company claims that they have resolved barriers with the help of a hybrid structure that connects the intermediary chains of public and private blockchain functions.

The platform also provides middleware that significantly reduces the technological entry barriers that game developers usually experience. Moreover, with its crowdfunding approaches, the development costs become lower and simplify the new users' entry experiences.

The ultimate goal of WEMIX is to attract the traditional gamers who are about one billion in number to attain mass adoption of blockchain-based games.

The token

WEMIX is the token of the play-to-earn (P2E) gaming platform WEMIX. It can be used to craft NFTs, traded, or won by players. It serves as currency in exchanging in-game tokens and is staked to earn rewards.

The top exchanges to buy and trade WEMIX are Bithumb, Korbit, Gate.io, Bybit, and OKX.

WEMIX Value Statistics (*subject to change*)

1 WEMIX– $3.45

1 WEMIX– 0.00008531 Bitcoin

1 WEMIX – 0.001146 ETH

Market Capitalization - **$425 million**

Fully diluted market cap - $ 3.5 billion

Circulating Supply – 1 23.2 million WEMIX

5. SushiSwap

The platform

SushiSwap is home to DeFi or decentralized finance. It is an AMM (automated market maker) that uses smart contracts to create markets for digital assets, hence allowing users to swap crypto.

This platform was a Uniswap fork that was launched in September 2020. It offers bigger rewards of in-house token SUSHI to network users and other enhanced features.

With the rapid growth of metaverse platforms, SushiSwap created an NFT marketplace, allowing its users to buy and sell digital products in a decentralized manner.

It was built by Chef Nomi and partners OxMaki and sushiwap. All three are pseudonymous entities who handled the business operations, product development, and SushiSwap code. Recently, the SushiSwap de-facto ownership was transferred to Sam Bankman-Friend, the CEO of FTX.

The token

SUSHI is the native currency of SushiSwap that offers an opportunity for users to vote on the community governance and get a cut of the exchange swap fee.

SUSHI Value Statistics (*subject to change*)

1 SUSHI– $3.30

1 SUSHI– 0.000077 Bitcoin

1 SUSHI – 0.001078 ETH

Market Capitalization - **$419.6 million**

Fully diluted market cap - $ 824.4million

Circulating Supply – 127.2 million SUSHI

6. Render Token

The platform

Render Token provides a GPU rendering network for various types of Metaverse projects. This brainchild of OTOY Incorporated CEO Jules Urbach aims to offer an open metaverse that puts the power of digital creation at your fingertips.

This project has revolutionized the rendering process and eliminated hardware limitations.

This powerful rending platform is powered by the Ethereum blockchain. It is now empowering the entertainment studious, artists, and startups, either by doing the work or connecting with mining partners who rent out their GPU capabilities

The token

The metaverse token of the network is **RNDR**. It was launched in 2020 at a price of $0.05. It is used to pay for the GPU compute power that node operators provide.

This token has a maximum supply of 536,870,012 units. It is available in Binance, Bitget, Bybit, Phemex, and FTX.

RNDR Value Statistics (*subject to change*)

1 RNDR– $1.70

1 RNDR– 0.00004204 Bitcoin

1 RNDR – 0.0005679 ETH

Market Capitalization - **$ 413.3 million**

Fully diluted market cap - $ 914.2 billion

Circulating Supply – 242.7 million RNDR

7. Illuvium

The platform

Illuvium is an Ethereum-based platform that fuses fantasy battle games and non-fungible tokens (NFTs). Players make a journey in the virtual landscape to find the creatures known as "illuvials".

This game provides entertainment to hardcore decentralized finance (DeFi) participants and traditional gamers who leverage its trading and collecting mechanisms.

In the early part of 2021, it has raised $5 million from investors including the venture capital company Framework Ventures.

It was built by more than 40 people who are working for the infrastructure's continuing development since 2020.

The worldwide team of industry experts includes the co-founders, game designer Aaron Warwick and brother Kieran Warwick who is a serial entrepreneur and crypto adopter.

Illuvium's 3D environment makes it unique from other games in the blockchain. It also has three outstanding features that set the platform apart.

This includes the Layer-2 Integration that scales up the applications with the functionality of NFT, the yield farming program, and the built-in DEX (decentralized exchange).

The token

ILV is the currency for Illuvium, the open-world RPG (role-playing game) on blockchain technology. It has various uses in the ecosystem:

- Rewards for in-game accomplishments

- Right to participate in the game governance via DAO (decentralized autonomous organization)

- Right of players to get a corresponding share of the Illuvium Vault

ILV Value Statistics (*subject to change*)

1 ILV– $519,35

1 ILV– 0.01338 Bitcoin

1 ILV – 0.1786 ETH

Market Capitalization - **$337.9 million**

Fully diluted market cap - $ 5,1 billion

Circulating Supply – 650.8 million ILV

8. PlayDapp

The platform

PlayDapp is a metaverse platform that promotes P2E game services. It has signed a partnership with IT Solutions for Business with the goal to enter the market of North America.

Other partners of PlayDapp are LINE and Samsung.

The token

PLA is the token of the PlayDapp ecosystem. It is used by participants to purchase and trade non-fungible tokens (NFTs). It can be earned as a reward for good performance in the game. The top crypto exchanges to buy and trade PLA are Crypto.com Exchange, Binance, Gate.io, Phemez, and BingX.

PLA Value Statistics (*subject to change*)

1 PLA– $0.8837

1 PLA– 0.00002116 Bitcoin

1 PLA – 0.0003085 ETH

Market Capitalization - **$320.6 million**

Fully diluted market cap - $ 618.6 million

Circulating Supply – 362.8 PLA

9. Ultra

The platform

Ultra provides a wide array of video games and gives them the opportunity to earn UOS. This entertainment publishing platform is a one-stop virtual world where users can discover different experiences with just a single log-in. This platform offers third-party game developers or companies to publish their entertainment services or apps and leverage their user base.

Moreover, it has two referral programs that offer bonuses that add a stream of income. One rewards the users who bring in new participants. The second one pays the gamers or influencers who promote the products, content, or platform.

The software downloading technology of Ultra lets gamers join beta tests, game curation, or watch advertisements.

The token

UOS is the native token used in the Ultra platform. You can buy virtual items and games, participate in various contests and tournaments, watch live streams, and interact with influencers in the industry.

UOS Value Statistics (*subject to change*)

1 UOS– $0.956

1 UOS– 0.00002345 Bitcoin

1 UOS – 0.0003127 ETH

Market Capitalization - **$ 270.8 million**

Fully diluted market cap - $ 961.5 billion

Circulating Supply – 283.3 million UOS

10. Vulcan Forged

The platform

From a humble beginning as a small non-fungible tokens platform, Vulcan Forged grew into a multi-dApp platform, marketplace, and gaming studio. It is now home to the 5 best NFT marketplaces in terms of sales volume, 20,000 communities, and 10 games.

The token

PYR is the token of Vulcan Forged. It is utilized by users to buy or sell virtual properties and stake in VulcanVerse lands or other digital assets. It can also be earned through play.

Other uses include payment for marketplace settlement, access to the NFT dApp incubation program and game developers, and sustaining/upgrading game asset levels. This coin reached its all-time high at $49.74 in December 2021.

PYR Value Statistics (*subject to change*)

1 PYR– $11.05

1 PYR– 0.0002962 Bitcoin

1 PYR – 0.003997 ETH

Market Capitalization - **$265.7 million**

Fully diluted market cap - $ 556 million

Circulating Supply – 23. 8 million PYR

11. Chromia

The platform

Chromia's ecosystem is designed to build the next-generation dApps and enhance the existing ones. The public standalone Layer-1 blockchain promotes improved data handling, scalability, and fee customization. Its programming language Rell helps developers code and program apps faster.

This type of language functions like SQL which promotes efficient storage and handling of data. It also helps in leveraging the immutability and security of the blockchain.

The blockchain that empowers Chromia features a unique relational architecture. It has a variety of DeFi applications, open-world farming games, and government land registries. Every dApp that runs on the network has its own sidechain that is connected with the primary blockchain.

With this setup, the developers can select their preferred fee structure like staking CHR to gain computational power or using the token as a transaction fee.

Chromia has also announced its $80 million Metaverse Grant Program together with Mines of Dalarnia and My Neighbor Alice.

In addition, the team behind the successful company launched its 2022 mentorship program to create the next level of blockchain innovation.

The token

CHR is the token of Chromia, the open-source blockchain and P2E platform founded by Swedish firm Chromaway AB. The token went public in May 2019. It is used by participants for various purposes like paying the hosting fees and staking in the platform.

In 2021, the increasing interest in the concept of metaverse bumped up the value of CHR to its all-time high of $1.50. It is available in Binance, Bybit, FTX, CoinTiger, and Phemex.

CHR Value Statistics (*subject to change*)

1 CHR– $0.418

1 CHR– 0.00001073 BTC

1 CHR – 0.0001329 ETH

Market Capitalization - **$ 237.3 million**

Fully diluted market cap - $ 418 million

Circulating Supply – 567.3 million CHR

12. YGG

The platform

Yield Guild Games (YGG) is a play-to-earn gaming ecosystem on a blockchain lending economy via a scholarship program of a decentralized autonomous organization (DAO). The platform invests in non-fungible tokens, then rents them to users who do not have capital fund. They can use the NFTs to earn in-game rewards.

The goal of the organization is to optimize its assets and share the revenues with the stakeholders, hence developing the biggest virtual economy in the world.

It was founded by the Manila-based company owned by Gabby Dizon and co-founded by Owl of Moistness and Beryl Li. These three comprise the team that launched Yearn Finance Community and Axie Infinity.

The token

YGG is the native token of Yield Guild Games. It allows the platform's investors to take part in the governance of the community. It is available in Binance, Phemex, Bybit, FTX, and OKX.

In 2021, the highest monthly direct revenue of YGG scholars was over $3.2 million. The maximum supply of YGG is 1 billion units.

About 45% of this total is set aside to support the community. It will be distributed gradually over a 4-year period. The remaining 40% is for the investors (24.9%), founders (15%), and the company's advisors/treasury (15%).

YGG Value Statistics (*subject to change*)

1 YGG– $ 1.85

1 YGG– 0.00005548 Bitcoin

1 YGG – 0.00073 ETH

Market Capitalization - **$210.9 million**

Fully diluted market cap - $ 1.8 billion

Circulating Supply – 113.9 million YGG

13. MyNeighborAlice

The platform

MyNeighborAlice is a metaverse game and a social platform. This project has an island concept theme, where users can collect NFTs, purchase virtual islands, and meet friends. To enjoy these experiences, you need to buy a plot of land with the platform's token ALICE. This cryptocurrency is also needed when improving the land, adding structures and vegetation, or buying in-game assets.

The token

Its metaverse token **ALICE** can be used in staking and is one of the best performing cryptocurrencies during the bullish trend. Its current market cap is more than $400 million.

ALICE Value Statistics (*subject to change*)

1 ALICE– $ 6.21

1 ALICE– 0.0001531 Bitcoin

1 ALICE – 0.002065 ETH

Market Capitalization - **$ 189.8 million**

Fully diluted market cap - $ 620.5 million

Circulating Supply – 30.6 million ALICE

14. Metahero

The platform

Metahero is designed to be software that allows the user to scan the body and convert it into a non-fungible token or NFT. In this form, it can be used in the metaverse platform as a personal avatar. It is the first of its kind in the industry as it promotes met-scanning or the realistic transformation of objects through scanning.

This metaverse platform went public in June 2021 with $10 million as initial funds. Using 3D technology to create virtual products and avatars, Metahero aims to catalyze the parallel worlds' evolution by bridging the gap between the physical and virtual ecosystems. One of its long-term plans is to install 12 3D chambers in various parts of the globe.

This would allow more than 100,000 objects or people to go through scanning and generate realistic avatars every single day.

The company was founded by Robert Gryn, a startup manager and serial tech entrepreneur who build multiple fast-growing firms in Europe. His partner is Piotr Harwas, the CEO of Wolf Studios who was behind the success of tech startups. This company is one of the largest providers of 3D scanners in the world.

Metahero's other project is Everdome, which allows the holders of HERO tokens to get discounts when they buy lands in the Everdone Metaverse. It is also associated with HEROSwap, the decentralized crypto exchange that offers token swapping, and the HERO App which helps users control the crypto funds.

The token

HERO is the native currency of the ecosystem. This metaverse token is used by users to pay for all the experiences in the platform like NFT sales, licensing, and scanning. With HERO, there will be more connections between gamers, artists, and entrepreneurs as the token's business use cases span across art and social media. Overall, the maximum supply of this token is 10 billion.

About 20% (2 billion) of them are locked in the liquidity pool, 10% (1 billion) will be sold in a public sale, 10% (1 billion) will be sold in a private sale, 10% (1 billion) will comprise the company reserve, and 30% (3 billion) will be utilized for marketing, strategic planning, and exchange listing. The remaining 20% (2 billion) is reserved for the Metahero team and advisors.

With more than 2.7 billion gamers across the world, the value of HERO has grown to $0.2518 five months after it went public. The top crypto exchanges to purchase META are CoinTiger, Gate.io, BingX, Bybit, and KuCoin.

HERO Value Statistics (*subject to change*)

1 HERO– $0.03329

1 HERO– 0.0000008226 Bitcoin

1 HERO – 0.00001105 ETH

Market Capitalization - **$169.6 million**

Fully diluted market cap - $ 332.8 million

Circulating Supply – 5.10 billion HERO

15. Bloktopia

The platform

Bloktopia project in the metaverse space is still in the infancy stage, but it has attracted the backing up of well-known investors. To name a few are Animoca Brands, Magnus Capital, Avalanche, ad AU21 Capital. It is also one of the selected projects that Polygon network support.

The selling point of Bloktopia is its state-of-the-art 3D creation engine that offers a real-time experience. This decentralized VR skyscraper offers 21 levels (to represent 21 million BTC). Each level delivers a unique experience to learn cryptocurrency, build networks, and acquire digital real estate property to earn revenue. To complete the infrastructure of every game level, users need to be creative and participative.

Moreover, Bloktopia has ADBLOK which is comprised of 84 small totems and 21 large totems on the skyscraper's first floor. They are ideal for advertising purposes. Sponsors and advertisers can leverage Bloktopia's growing userbase through its dedicated NFT mechanism.

It plans to develop a WWE (World Wrestling Entertainment) space and develop new mechanisms that would enable the users to generate income and content.

The token

BLOK is the utility token of Bloktopia. It is used to buy real estate assets in NFT form. When it is staked, it can yield up to 60% profit annually. Holders of this token are called Bloktopians. They use BLOK to procure income streams through land possession, assembling organizations, promoting income, and earning game rewards.

This token unlocks exclusive privileges like voting right in the metaverse governance, buying advertising space, creating a customized metaverse version, and purchasing avatars.

It has a total supply of 200 million which is distributed to different stakeholders and activities. BLOK can be bought and traded in Gate.io, Bitget, Bitrue, KuCoin, and OKX.

BLOK Value Statistics (*subject to change*)

1 BLOK– $0.01385

1 BLOK– 0.000000396 Bitcoin

1 BLOK – 0.000005261 ETH

Market Capitalization - **$115.4 million**

Fully diluted market cap - $ 2.7 billion

Circulating Supply – 8.34 billion BLOK

16. WILD (Wilder World)

The platform

Wilder World is the first 5D metaverse project that is developing its platform on its their own. This wide-scale endeavor involves allowing the users to purchase, build, or create in-game items in the form of tradable NFTs. Powered by the Ethereum blockchain, users can make customized condos, land, and other structures.

The token

The native token of Wilder World is **WILD**. It is used within the platform's marketplace to purchase NFTs including 5D vehicles, art pieces, modern condos, or plots of land. By holding these tokens, you become an official Wilder World platform. You get unlimited access to internal incentives and rewards within the metaverse.

WILD Value Statistics (*subject to change*)

1 WILD– $1.09

1 WILD– 0.00002875 Bitcoin

1 WILD – 0.00028681 ETH

Market Capitalization - **$ 92.6 million**

Fully diluted market cap - $ 543.4 million

Circulating Supply – 85.2 million WILD

17. Red Fox Labs

The platform

RedFOX Labs was established in 2018. This internet-technology company works to identify and create business models for various markets in Southeast Asia. It aims to become the leading metaverse platform that will provide immersive experiences in gaming, retail shopping, media, and rewards.

The token

RFOX is the token of the RedFOX Labs. It is used by participants to purchase lands and virtual assets. The maximum supply of this token will be 2 billion units. It is available in PancakeSwap (V2), Gate.io, KuCoin, Uniswap (V3), and Bitget.

RFOX Value Statistics (*subject to change*)

1 RFOX– $0.04387

1 RFOX– 0.00000182 Bitcoin

1 RFOX – 0.00001568 ETH

Market Capitalization - **$ 57.6 million**

Fully diluted market cap - $ 87.8 million

Circulating Supply – 1.31 billion RFOX

18. Somnium Space

The platform

Somnium Space is an open-source VR platform where users can own plots of land, buildings, homes, and NFTs. Users are also allowed to create their own scenes and deploy human-like avatars. With multiple opportunities and mind-boggling virtual experiences to try, this metaverse project is incredibly unique and fun.

With colorful graphics and customizable spaces and avatars, it allows users to combine the functionalities of communication, entertainment, e-commerce, and more.

Moreover, its WebXR platform makes it easy for users to access their properties using any device. This multichain approach becomes possible with the use of the Polygon blockchain which aims to eliminate the entry barriers that global users typically encounter. The ability of Somnium Space to seamlessly integrate the non-fungible tokens in the metaverse has attracted the interest of the NFT industry.

This lets the users enjoy new activities like creating their own NFT Gallery, making new NFT-based experiences or worlds, dancing with a tracking kit, or attending VR events via your avatar.

The token

CUBE is the native token of Somnium Space. It works to fuel the virtual ecosystem and make the asset transfer within the metaverse smooth. The popular exchanges to purchase and trade CUBES stock are CoinEx, Gemini, and Bitget.

1 CUBE– $4.47

1 CUBE– 0.000116 Bitcoin

1 CHR – 0.001659 ETH

Market Capitalization - **$ 55.8 million**

Fully diluted market cap - $ 446.4 million

Circulating Supply – 12.5 billion CUBE

19. Highstreet

The platform

Highstreet is a platform that allows gamers to explore, fight monsters, and complete quests in the metaverse. Using its native token HIGH, you can shop digital items in the platform's marketplace and in Shopify stores that are integrated into the game. Users can also acquire digital in-game items and exchange them for real-life goods.

Aside from HIGH, it has another token called STREET that can be acquired after completing the game tasks. It is a utility token that can be used to pay for travel tickets and hotel accommodation, buy weapons and armors, or facilitate gaming commerce. All NFTs on the platform is divided into two fractions.

It is founded by Jenny Gou and Travis Wu. Gou is an award-winning film producer of virtual reality, entrepreneur, and art collector. Wu is a well-known software developer with a VR background and a strong interest in blockchain. They have rebranded the computer vision LumiereVR to Highstreet, a company that focuses on enhancing the retail experience of users by incorporating VR technology.

In the context of what the metaverse promises, Highstreet has shown the seamless traverse from the real world to the meta world. This metaverse project is a good option for investors whose measure of success of the concept is practicality. It is also backed by HTC, a reputable tech company in the industry.

The token

HIGH is the native currency of Highstreet, a decentralized P2E, commerce-centered metaverse with VR support. It is the platform's governance token that gives rights to users to be part of the major decisions by casting a vote.

This token was launched in October 2021 and used to gain profit by staking or buying items from the marketplace. It can be obtained by participating in the special events of the metaverse and is paid to the property owners in the form of taxes. HIGH is available in Binance, Crypto.com Exchange, Phemex, Gate.io, Bitget, Uniswap (V2), LBank, PancakeSwap, and HOO.

HIGH Value Statistics (*subject to change*)

1 HIGH– $4.36

1 HIGH– 0.0001081 Bitcoin

1 HIGH – 0.001453 ETH

Market Capitalization - **$54 million**

Fully diluted market cap - $ 438.9 million

Circulating Supply – 12.3 million HIGH

20. Star Atlas

The platform

Star Atlas is a web-based multiplayer game in the virtual reality realm. This metaverse project is powered by Solana on Unreal Engine 5, allowing the users to experience a real-time and cinema-quality environment. The game features abundant stars for exploitation and exploration. It is a role-playing game where participants can create revenue streams and mine digital resources. Acquired in-game assets can be redeemed for fiat currency. What makes Star Atlas unique is its capability to provide several genres that bring a more immersive experience to the metaverse.

It offers simultaneous options to explore and form alliances with other gamers, battle against other players to get digital assets or earn through staking the tokens. Star Atlas has another token-POLIS which acts as the governance token of the platform.

The token

ATLAS is the metaverse tokens of Star Atlas. It has a maximum supply of 36 billion coins with more than 2 billion in circulation. The crypto exchanges to buy and trade ATLAS are Gate.io, Bitget, MEXC, and FTX. It can be sued to buy in-game assets and non-fungible tokens on the NFT marketplace.

ATLAS Value Statistics (*subject to change*)

1 ATLAS– $0.02102

1 ATLAS– 0.0000005264 Bitcoin

1 ATLAS – 0.000007071 ETH

Market Capitalization - **$ 45 million**

Fully diluted market cap - $ 758.6 million

Circulating Supply – 2.16 billion ATLAS

Takeaways

- At this juncture, there is a rapid growth of Metaverse as big players in tech and non-tech industries are upgrading their platform infrastructures.

- Check out our list of the best platforms to consider this 2022 if you want to be part of the pioneer investors who believe in the potentials of the Metaverse.

Aside from these popular platforms, you can also leverage the potential of the new and upcoming projects this year. The list is on the final chapter.

Chapter 9

Creating Wealth in Metaverse:

Strategy 4-Invest in New and Upcoming Projects

"Metaverse is not only a place to game. The future world is photorealistic."-
Jensen Huang

We are now living in a transformative time, where the exciting potentials and experiences in the virtual realm are slowly unfolding. All the talks about the concepts of cryptocurrency, blockchain, Web 3.0, and the Metaverse have manifested into a reality.

At this stage of the Metaverse development, a lot of aspects of this concept are still abstract. However, there are already components that play a foundation role like the NFTs, cryptocurrencies, and blockchain technology. Companies are now investing in Web 3.0

technologies and building their mainstream activities online

From this year onward, the primary market is the enterprises. Developers of the Metaverse will be working to provide new technology applications with enhanced features and products. There will be more startups that focus on niche solutions that revolve around virtual reality, collaboration, and data visualization.

Chapter summary

- Classification of Metaverse projects
- List of most promising Metaverse projects
- Takeaways

Classification of Metaverse projects

To reiterate, the Metaverse project is a computer-generated space. This highly-immersive, 3D parallel universe is focused on providing real-world-like social interactions and activities. Users have their own avatars to represent their virtual identity to engage with other players or participants.

There are two primary classifications of Metaverse:

1. **Blockchain-based Metaverse** - It is a platform that delivers real-world value to the virtual space through non-fungible tokens (NFTs), blockchain, and decentralized finance (DeFi) technologies. Examples are Axies Infinity, Decentraland, and The Sandbox.

2. **Collaborative virtual environment** – It is a virtual world where users gather and collaborate for recreation, entertainment, or business purposes. Examples of this type of Metaverse are Facebook, Roblox, and Fortnite.

List of most promising Metaverse projects

RedFox

The platform

RedFox is a startup technology company that is developing a standalone Metaverse ecosystem that is focused on retail, gaming, media, finance, NFTS, and rewards. It aims to create a lavish virtual shopping mall that anyone can access via phone or computer.

Its focal point is RFOX VALT, a fully- immersive VR experience that is designed to bring solutions to the essential industries in the Metaverse.

- RFOX Media allows users to monetize their content, earn rewards by doing participative contributions, or playing the games.

- RFOX Games is a tournament-based environment with a play-to-earn P2E system. Users have access to a variety of games.

- RFOX NFTs let businesses develop their own non-fungible tokens on the platform.

- RFOX Finance empowers the holders of the tokens to utilize the platform's services and DeFi products for their revenue streams.

The token

The multichain metaverse token of RedFox is RFOX. It fuels the Metaverse ecosystem and its technology. It can be purchased from Binance Smart Chain, Ethereum, and WAX.

RFOX Value Statistics (*subject to change*)

1 RFOX– $0.414

1 RFOX– 0.000001046 Bitcoin

1 RFOX – 0.00001415 ETH

Market Capitalization - $ **52.6 million**

Fully diluted market cap - $ 80.2 million

Circulating Supply – 1.31 billion RFOX

Dotmoovs

The platform

Dotmoovs is a play-to-earn (P2E) mobile application that enables users to compete by performing a dance, sports, or more to earn rewards. It is like a crypto version of the popular TikTok. It allows peer-to-peer competition where users can challenge each other and win pot tokens. Dotmoovs has a proprietary AI algorithm that scores movements and sports tricks based on your recorded video.

It is in its early stage, which makes it a highly viable investment. Dotmoovs has iOS and Android apps that can be downloaded, making it more accessible to global users. This Metaverse platform has the most exclusive NFT collection of athletes as it continues its mission to revolutionize the traditional way of sports competition.

The token

Its metaverse crypto coin is **MOOV**, which is a fast-rising cryptocurrency. This token is used to buy NFTs and as rewards. It can be purchased and traded in PancakeSwap (V2), Gate.io, MEXC, and BitGlobal.

Polychain Monsters

The platform

Polychain Monsters is a Metaverse crypto game that features the Pokemon-inspired Polymons. They are non-fungible token (NFT) creatures that are animated art. For Pokemon fans, this game is for you. It was launched during the middle of the NFT craze in the first quarter of 2021.

With the perfect combination of modern technology and nostalgia of the '90s trading popularity of Pokemon cards, Polymon Monsters has successfully placed itself in the crypto space. It has also secured the backing and $740,000 funding from 6 major investors including the Morningstar Ventures and Moonrock Capital.

Developers of this Metaverse project are set to unveil other interesting features to boost the gaming experiences of users. It includes PMON staking, cross-chain support with Polkadot, and level-2 meta-data properties full utilization.

The token

Users can buy Polychain Monster's NFT booster packs using the platform's native utility token **PMON**. If you are lucky, you get a rare Polymon that is included in the pack. PMON is the native currency of this platform, which is an ETH-20 token. You can buy this token on Gate.io, MEXC, LBank, PancakeSwap, KuCoin, SushiSwap, Hoo, and more.

PMON Value Statistics (*subject to change*)

1 PMON– $ 3.77

1 PMON– 0.00009302 Bitcoin

1 PMON – 0.001255 ETH

Market Capitalization - $ 12.6 million

Fully diluted market cap - $ 34.5 million

Circulating Supply – 3.4 million PMON

Mogul Productions

The platform

Mogul Productions was launched in April 2021 and established itself as a DeFiFi (decentralized film financing) and a platform for NFTs. This Metaverse project offers a Launchpad for filmmakers and entertainment professionals who want to get funding by connecting financiers, creators, and movie fans.

Users of the platform can submit movie scripts and get a chance to produce them into movies. It also rewards participation and engagement in various experiences with STARS.

There is a growing Mogul community that is composed of film enthusiasts. People become a Mogul once they sign up to the platform.

Mogul Productions come with a global NFT dashboard and a decentralized finance (DeFi) platform. You can discover non-fungible tokens of Hollywood iconic figures and buy them from the official marketplace of the platform.

The project's major selling point is the robust partnership with the big names in the cryptocurrency space such as Chainlink, ApeSwap, Polygon, CEEK VR, and a lot more.

The advisors and teams behind this innovative project are award-winning directors, scriptwriters, actors, and producers in Hollywood.

The token

Its utility crypto is called **STARS**, the currency that allows users to purchase NFTs, submit scripts, and engage in other activities.

It is available on PancakeSwap, Uniswap (V2), MEXC, LATOKEN, Decoin, and other crypto exchanges.

STARS Value Statistics (*subject to change*)

1 STARS– $0.04481

1 STARS– 0.000001107 Bitcoin

1 STARS – 0.00001495 ETH

Market Capitalization - $ **13.7 million**

Fully diluted market cap - $ 17.9 million

Circulating Supply – 306.6 million STARS

Nakamoto Games

The platform

Nakamoto Games is a P2E platform that offers crypto games. It has a variety of games that bring earnings to players and investors of the tokens. Its ecosystem is evolving to provide a premier platform.

It will soon launch the in-house suite of games where developer can easily deploy their creations and players get a chance to compete to get rewards and weekly prize pool.

Its plan to introduce the NAKAverse places Nakamoto Games on the list of companies venturing into the metaverse.

Investors and players can leverage the power of its real in-game economy and purchase land, build structures, and do a lot more.

The token

NAKA is the platform's native token. It is vital to the P2E ecosystem of the Nakamoto Games as it provides the access to enter the ecosystem. The token is the heart of this gaming platform.

It can also be earned from the weekly prize pool where highest-ranking gamers share the rewards. Moreover, holders of NAKA can also participate on major decisions in the platform's governance.

NAKA Value Statistics (*subject to change*)

1 NAKA– $0.3042

1 NAKA– 0.000007536 Bitcoin

1 NAKA – 0.001017 ETH

Market Capitalization - $ **9.6 million**

Fully diluted market cap - $ 54.7 million

Circulating Supply – 31.5 million NAKA

Cryptovoxels

The platform

Cryptovoxels is a metaverse built on top of the Ethereum blockchain. This gaming platform is leveraging the metaverse potential by providing a unique world of NFTs and great adventures. Its creator is the Nolan Consulting, a New Zealand-based game development firm. This virtual universe mixes gaming and decentralized finance (DeFi).

The game concept of Cryptovoxels simulates the experiences in the real world. It integrates real-world events and products. In this Metaverse, players can build their stores, create NFT art galleries, purchase virtual land, make avatars, play games on the platform, and interact with other users.

The token

Tokens of this platform are **CVPA** (Cryptovoxels Parcel), an NFT that represents the Origin City land. It is not listed on crypto trading platform, but can be purchased on OpenSea which is the official secondary marketplace of the game. Also, users of the platform can get hold of CVPA during the weekly auction on Cryptovoxels.

Silks

The platform

The Silks ecosystem went public in June, 2021. Its upcoming Metaverse project "Games of Silks" is highly-anticipated as it will be taking the P2E games to another level by offering a feature-packed, thoroughbred horse-racing-inspired platform.

Within this virtual world, users can buy and own their own Silks horses that are represented as NFTs. With a self-sustaining marketplace, the participants can smoothly trade their horses.

What makes it more exciting is that the virtual Silks horses are linked to the horses in the real world. This allows players to access the database that offers information on the bloodline of the thoroughbred, growth history and results of previous racing experiences. Verification of the data is done through the PoS (Proof-of-Stake) consensus mechanism.

The token

STT is Silks' native token. It can be used by users as in-game currency to purchase Silks horses, avatars, stables, and plots of land. It can also be earned as a staking reward when the real-world horses win their races. Another way to earn STT is to breed horses when the physical counterpart of their virtual horse retired, becoming a stallion or a broodmare. Professional Silks player can also monetize their skills via "pinhooking" or profiting from buying and selling horses before their first real-world competition.

The governance token of Silks metaverse is SLK. Holders of this currency automatically become a member of the Silks DAO and have the right to cast their vote on the platform's major decisions. Moreover, users can convert the STT tokens to SLK.

Memoverse

The platform

Memoverse is a platform that offers unique Learn-2-Earn and Memorize-2-Earn systems. It is the Web 3.0 virtual vaults or Memory Palaces that store human memory. This memorization gamified platform comes with its proprietary decentralized finance (DeFi) instruments and non-fungible tokens (NFT) marketplace.

The premise of Memoverse is turning memorization into a game so the process becomes more fun and effective. The game is inspired by Sherlock Holmes' technique of creating a 'mind palace' to keep and retrieve virtually all information he needs. It is also a popular approach of memory champions who are advocates of memorization.

The main launching of this Memoverse Play-to-Earn platform will be on the 3rd or 4th quarter of 2022.

The token

The native token of Memoverse is MEMO. It can be earned by competing in memorization contests or creating/owning memory palaces. The token can be used to buy in-game assets and NFTs that can be sold or traded on the platform's marketplace.

Bit.Country

The platform

Bit.Country is a portal that allows businesses and non-technical users to create their own metaverse according to their needs. Developers can use the network's API, allowing the smart contract users to customize and personalize their virtual world by minting digital art and digital real estate. Its framework is designed for more immersive 3D experiences, combining a polygon system with a voxel world. It takes pride in being the mother of user-generated Metaverses.

The token

The metaverse token of Bit.Country is NUUM. Its launching is widely-anticipated as it is the means to buy a parcel of land on the platform. There will be 100,000 parcels that can be used for content creation, events, advertising, or branding purposes.

Pegaxy

The platform

Pegaxy is an NFT-based, free P2E horse racing game platform. This metaverse allows users to enter their Pega (inspired by the mythical creature Pegasus) into PvP or player-versus-player races and win VIS rewards. The horses are available to those who want to buy, breed, sell, or rent them.

It is now available on desktops and the official launch on Android and iOS is set for the second quarter of 2022. What makes Pegaxy unique is that it lets users join the metaverse without shelling an initial investment. Its rental system is automated with a profit-sharing model agreement that includes predetermined conditions. The Grand Dash Tournament is the most anticipated annual competition in this metaverse. To qualify, players should win monthly qualification rounds.

The token

The utility token of Pegaxy is VIS (Vigorus) while its governance token is PGX (Pegaxy Stone). VIS serves as the primary money to facilitate commerce transactions within the game. It can also be earned as reward money. PGX holders can use participate in stacking for-profit and voting for the major proposals of the network's owners.

Takeaways

- Study the background and potential of every new Metaverse project in the market.

- Make sure that the companies behind these new projects are stable and have a good reputation.

Chapter 10

Creating Wealth in Metaverse:

Strategy 5-Leverage the Opportunities of Real Estate

"There are big risks, but potentially big rewards." - Jannie Yorio, Republic Realm CEO

There will be a boom in the virtual estate, where lands sell for millions of dollars. Land in the Metaverse is a lucrative, long-term investment that will give you a steady flow of passive income. Moreover, the property will also grow in value and you can sell higher than your investment.

Chapter summary

- Ways to earn in Metaverse real estate
- How to buy land in the Metaverse?
- Takeaways

In 2021, real estate sales of "Big Four"-Decentraland, Sandbox, Somnium, and Cryptovoxels was $502 million. It is expected that the numbers will be larger this 2022 and beyond.

Ways to earn in metaverse real estate

For those who are interested in real estate jobs, the following are good opportunities.

Brokering

Real estate companies will need more brokers to handle the properties for sale or lease. You can enjoy generous commissions by connecting sellers and buyers. Another way is to offer your consultancy or advice as a professional real estate broker.

Flipping

You can buy lands and digital properties and then resell them to interested people who want to own a digital land in the metaverse. Becoming a landlord gives you regular passive income.

Property Management

If you have previous experience in managing other people's property, monetize your expertise by becoming a virtual property manager. You can also apply as an administrator of virtual lands, buildings, or entertainment venues in the metaverse.

Renting out property

Like in the physical world, renting out your house or plot of land brings income. If your virtual property is located in a high traffic area, use it for advertising purposes. You can create virtual shopping malls, casinos, boutiques, hotels, and other *entertainment* centers.

Make a profit by charging people or selling digital goods or services. You can also sell or rent part of the building, sell ads space, or charge admission fees.

Designing

One of the lucrative jobs in the Metaverse is 3D designing. The digital world needs creative people who will conceptualize and bring the land into life by creating structures.

If you are a professional designer or graphic artist, joining a company or freelancing your services is a good option.

Investing in Real Estate

MREIT or MetaSpace Real Estate Investment Trust offers people an opportunity to invest in profitable real estate properties in the Metaverse. Just like the traditional trust, you can buy shares in their projects.

How to buy land in the Metaverse

Step 1: Set up a digital wallet to hold your cryptocurrency.

Step 2: Select the buying platform where you want to buy property.

Step 3: Make an offer and close the deal.

Takeaways

- A real estate property in the Metaverse promises a good return on investment.

- Virtual land offers a multitude of income-generating opportunities.

Conclusion

Thank you for reading my book "**Metaverse Investing Guide for Beginners**: *Top 5 Unique Strategies to Create Wealth in Metaverse. Why Metaverse Will Create More Millionaires Than Anything Else.*

If you're here with me right now, I know that you are yearn for more learning about this incredible concept called Metaverse. Hence, I would like to encourage you to keep digesting the investing information that I have shared with you.

Investing, in general, is both a rewarding and challenging endeavor. Since it involves money, time, and effort, we need to be careful where to place our trust. Not all Metaverse players are cut with the same goals, values, and business models.

As the race to become the top providers of ultimate Metaverse platforms continue, it is up to us to keep learning and become familiar with this idea of a future world. At present, major corporations are cashing in cryptocurrency and eyeing the proprietary tokens of the early

Metaverse players as well as non-fungible tokens (NFTs).

The Metaverse niche is very attractive to startups and existing companies that have experienced the life-changing benefits of investing in digital assets. One thing is sure, the people behind the businesses have insights that trigger them to be on the line before the boom of Metaverse. This has happened in Bitcoin. And look how early investors turned to become billionaires and millionaires during the bull season.

But as I said, there is no exact timeline for the real world and Metaverse convergence will occur. It can be soon or much longer, but the enthusiasm of stakeholders has already set the grinding motion.

You can start your journey to the Metaverse by investing in NFTs, crypto tokens, blockchain projects, and Metaverse-related products. Or you may use your creative talents to earn passive income and then invest them in Metaverse real estate property.

Again, my sincere appreciation for taking the time to read **Metaverse Investing Guide for Beginners**: *Top 5 Unique Strategies to Create Wealth in Metaverse. Why Metaverse Will Create More Millionaires Than Anything Else.*

I wish you well and see you, next MILLIONAIRE!